31 DAYS
OF WISDOM
FOR COUPLES

A STUDY THROUGH THE BOOK OF PROVERBS

THOMAS AND LYSANDRA
OSTERKAMP

ALSO BY THOMAS AND LYSANDRA OSTERKAMP

Balancing the Crazy
Happily Never After

31 DAYS
OF WISDOM
FOR COUPLES

A STUDY THROUGH THE BOOK OF PROVERBS

THOMAS AND LYSANDRA
OSTERKAMP

Contents

Introduction   8

Week 1: Proverbs 1–7   12

Week 2: Proverbs 8–14   44

Week 3: Proverbs 15–21   84

Week 4: Proverbs 22–28   126

Week 5: Proverbs 29–31   164

Conclusion   182

Introduction

If you have entered into marriage, the most sacred of all earthly relationships, you know that it isn't for the faint of heart. Marriage is not easy. It's the most challenging covenant you will ever be a part of. To simply stay together for decades is a huge accomplishment these days, let alone to have a marriage you both enjoy and cherish.

A healthy and cheerful marriage relationship is rare and special. The only way to experience this kind of relationship with your spouse is to be wise in how you live and the way you interact with each other. You cannot have an awesome marriage relationship without wisdom.

Wisdom is the answer to your relationship goals. Thankfully, there is a place we can go to find wisdom for all of life's situations, the book of Proverbs. Proverbs was written primarily by King Solomon who was the wisest man to ever live. Overall, the purpose of the book of Proverbs is to provide wisdom for us.

God knew that there would be numerous times in our lives where we wouldn't know what to do or how to handle situations and interpersonal relationships. So, He provided a place we could go to find the wisdom we need to make good choices, say the right words, and conduct ourselves in a way that we won't regret.

As you begin this journey through Proverbs, prepare your hearts together through prayer. Ask God to show you, through this book of wisdom, areas in your life where you aren't walking in wisdom. Talk to God's Holy Spirit about how you can change. Be open to how He leads you in this study. Enjoy time in the Word and with your spouse.

Pray Psalm 25:5 as you begin this journey through Proverbs together, *"Lead me in your truth and teach me, for you are the God of my salvation; for you I wait all the day long."*

Day 1: Proverbs Chapter 1

Marriage Goal: Obtain wisdom as a couple.

"The fear of the Lord is the beginning of knowledge;
fools despise wisdom and instruction."

Proverbs 1:7

Recognize Your Need for Wisdom

The first step to obtaining wisdom is understanding that you don't have it (*"fools despise wisdom and instruction."*). You don't have it because you aren't searching for it—you believe you already have it.

Proverbs Chapter 1 tells us that *"The fear of the Lord is the beginning of knowledge."* This is true in all aspects of life, including your marriage. People often misunderstand "the fear of the Lord." Am I supposed to be terrified of God striking me dead every time I mess up? Is that the fear of the Lord? Many people live their lives afraid of the "big guy in the sky." This is not what the fear of the Lord is.

The fear of the Lord is having a proper reverence for God, who He is, and how great He is. When we have an appropriate reverence and respect for Him, this leads to us respecting everything He says and how He leads us. The result of reverencing His Word and living it is wisdom. A life lived in wisdom is a blessed and happy life! When we live according to God's wisdom, we save ourselves from the unnecessary hurt and pain of bad choices.

There are many places in Scripture that talk about the fear of the Lord as the beginning of wisdom. Psalm 111:10 shares the benefits of having a proper fear of God, *"The fear of the Lord is the beginning of wisdom; all those who practice it have a good understanding. His praise endures forever!"*

Fearing the Lord isn't about being afraid of Him at all, but rather understanding He holds the secrets of a peaceful life and allowing that to dictate how we live. His way isn't just about rules and restrictions to make us miserable. God's way provides boundaries, giving us an optimal experience on this earth and allowing us to store up treasure in eternity.

Knowledge and wisdom go hand in hand, and both are vital in a healthy marriage relationship. Knowledge is knowing information; wisdom is allowing that knowledge to affect your behavior.

Thomas

Men, knowledge in marriage is understanding your wife and allowing the knowledge you have of her to affect your interactions with her. I know what you are thinking, "Can a man ever understand a woman?" Not only can you, but you are commanded to know and understand your wife in 1 Peter 3:7, *"Likewise, husbands, live with your wives in an understanding way ..."*

One thing I know about my wife is that when she shares frustrations with me, she needs me to listen to her. I know that she doesn't really want me to fix her problems, she wants a sounding board. She wants me to empathize with her.

This knowledge should affect my behavior, resulting in wise action. So, when she vents her frustrations with me, I sit quietly, listen, and react appropriately to what she says. This is wisdom in marriage.

If I don't put the knowledge that I have of my wife into action, I hear her venting to me and immediately begin to tell her how to fix the situation. I tell her she shouldn't be upset, but to simply follow my plan to remedy her circumstance. This is not wise. If you've been married for very long, you know it's never wise to tell your wife she shouldn't be upset and that you know how to fix everything.

Lysandra

Ladies, knowledge is understanding that your husband doesn't comprehend information given to him during his favorite team's game. If I have no wisdom, I will sit next to Thomas on the couch as he's watching the Hawkeyes play football and pull out my phone calendar. I will then inform him of my upcoming schedule, the girls' schedule, and his schedule. I'll add to this explaining that I need him to pick the girls up from their college class tomorrow. He will nod in robotic agreement followed by a very loud outburst directed at the referees.

We all know men enough to know what's going to happen tomorrow, right? The girls are going to be standing outside then call me and ask where Daddy is. Yes, I had to learn this the hard way. Experience leads to future wisdom too!

In this same scenario, if I would have acted on the knowledge I have about my husband, I would have patiently waited until the game was over to ask him to pick the kids up from school tomorrow. Wisdom also dictates I send him a reminder text an hour before pickup time as well.

Wisdom Comes from God

If you want wisdom in your marriage, and we're assuming you do since you bought this book, you're on the right path. However, this book isn't your path to wisdom; God is your path to wisdom. He holds all wisdom as the Creator of all that exists.

Look at the promise that James wrote in James 1:5, *"If any of you lacks wisdom, let him ask of God, who gives generously to all without reproach, and it will be given Him."*

Go to God and ask for wisdom in every aspect of your life, including your marriage. Ask Him for wisdom in how you speak to your spouse, how you treat them, the things you do, and the way you think about them. This person you married is the most precious, God-given gift to you in the world. This is your MVP, most valuable person. Ask God to give you a greater understanding of your spouse. He will answer your prayer, and you will have a sweeter relationship because of it.

Make it Personal:

1. How have you interpreted the fear of the Lord in the past?

2. What does a proper reverence for God lead you to do?

3. Share a time you didn't act in wisdom toward your spouse.

4. Describe something you know about your spouse and how you can use wisdom in that area.

5. Each of you take a moment to pray out loud, asking God for wisdom in your marriage.

Day 2: Proverbs Chapter 2

Marriage Goal: Don't wait for wisdom to come to you, go search for it together.

"Yes, if you call out for insight and raise your voice for understanding, if you seek it like silver and search for it as for hidden treasures, then you will understand the fear of the Lord and find the knowledge of God. For the Lord gives wisdom; from his mouth come knowledge and understanding."

Proverbs 2:3–6

Hidden Treasures

It would be nice to walk along and discover a pot of gold, but we all know that's probably not going to happen. You won't accidentally stumble upon wisdom either. You must search for it and pursue it. Think of the way you pursued your spouse before they were your spouse. You learned about them—you became a student of them. You spent every moment you could with them. You called, texted, emailed, Facetimed, walked, talked, and whatever else you could do to be near them. You soaked up information about them like a sponge. They were your treasure, and you loved the treasure hunt!

Wisdom must be pursued as the treasure it is. We must go after it by studying the Word of God, studying Jesus, praying for it, and seeking it from other reliable godly sources.

Thomas

When Lysandra and I were engaged to be married, we wanted to do everything we possibly could to have a great marriage. We were doing all the right things in preparation for our wedding. We had pre-marital counseling with the pastor of my church, we participated in a marriage mentoring program with her church, and we completed our own marriage study using Christian pre-marital books. We pursued marital wisdom from anywhere and everywhere that we could. We wanted the knowledge experienced couples had. We had a great start by the time we walked down the aisle. But we needed more.

Lysandra

After marriage, we began to coast a little. We felt like we had the information we needed and now we could just chill "till death do us part." That's when a lot of discontentment in our relationship began. We soon learned we needed some help. We began to look for couples who had been married longer than we had and spent time with them. We asked questions and learned from their example. We knew that we couldn't stop pursuing wisdom and instruction. It must be a lifelong pursuit.

Even after marriage we must continue to be students of wisdom and instruction. We now know we need to continuously study the Bible, read marriage books, and go to marriage conferences and retreats. We have been married now for over twenty years, and we are still looking for more wisdom and instruction for our life and for our marriage.

Chasing Something

You are chasing something. Your spouse is chasing something. Each of you have priorities and goals. Are your priorities and goals the best ones? Are you pursuing wisdom as the treasure it is?

Make it Personal:

1. What pre-marital counseling did you take to prepare for your marriage?

2. In what ways did you pursue your spouse when you were dating?

3. How have you pursed wisdom together since you got married?

4. Name some couples you know who seem to have successful marriages defined by wisdom.

5. How will you as a couple chase after wisdom in the next year?

Day 3: Proverbs Chapter 3

Marriage Goal: Do good to your spouse.

"Do not withhold good from those to whom it is due, when it is in your power to do it. Do not say to your neighbor, 'Go, and come again, tomorrow I will give it'—when you have it with you."

Proverbs 3:27–28

Do Good to Your Neighbor

There is no closer neighbor to you than the one you wake up next to every morning. Your spouse is your closest neighbor.

Why is it the hardest to self-sacrifice for people who are the closest to us? It's almost easier to do good to an acquaintance than our spouse. We say, "I'll take a bullet for you," but we won't go downstairs and get our spouse a glass of water.

Often in a marriage relationship, it seems we base doing good to each other on the good they've done to us. I won't do good to you if you haven't been good to me. You only get what you deserve. This passage is not about what the other person deserves. If you have the power to do good, do it. That's all.

We often don't want to do good to our spouse when it means we experience discomfort or inconvenience—sometimes it's simply because we're lazy.

Lysandra

The other day I had been out working all day. I was tired on my way home. Thomas texted me, "Hey babe, I'm about to start a mentoring session, will you stop on your way home and grab some frozen pizzas for supper? I'll pop mine in the oven after my session is over."

I thought, "Ugh! I don't want to make a stop. I'm tired and gross." I had no reason not to stop other than that I was tired and feeling lazy. After a minor fight in my mind between kind Lysandra and lazy Lysandra, I texted back. "Sure, I'm going right by the grocery store. What kind do you want?"

Thomas

I knew Lysandra had worked all day and was tired. I knew there was a chance she would say no, and I would have understood. I just really felt like a Digiorno stuffed-crust supreme pizza! It tasted so good too. It meant a lot to me that my wife sacrificed her time and energy for me, even after a long, hard day. She did something good to me despite how she felt, and it spoke volumes to me.

Fight the Urge to Say No

When your spouse asks you to do something nice for them, fight the urge to say no. There will always be reasons to say no: I don't want to, I'm tired, I'm comfortable, it's not on my way, I worked more than you today, it's difficult, I did it last time, and so many more! Don't give into those reasons, no matter how legitimate they are. If you have the power to do good to your spouse, do it. Say yes!

Doing good can go above and beyond saying yes when they ask you to do something for them. Go the extra mile whenever you can. Even if they don't ask for something, recognize when you can bless them with some good. It's not about the big and extravagant gestures or gifts. It's the everyday, regular situations where you can support your spouse and speak love to them. Do the chore, run the errand, get the blanket for them, help with the kids, buy them their favorite treat, and rub their feet, especially when they don't ask you for it.

You are wise when you go above and beyond in doing good to your spouse. You will experience a loving and beautiful marriage relationship.

Make it Personal:

1. What prevents you from doing good to your spouse?

2. Why do you think it's sometimes easier to do good to those whom we aren't related to?

3. Name three good things your spouse has done for you recently.

4. How do you feel when your spouse does good to you?

5. List three good things you will do for your spouse this week.

Day 4: Proverbs Chapter 4

Marriage Goal: Protect your heart at all costs.

"Keep your heart with all vigilance, for from it flow the springs of life."

Proverbs 4:23

A Dangerous Entity

Have you ever heard someone say that a person has a good heart? This really isn't true. In fact, none of us do. At our natural core we are selfish, sinful human beings. Beware of the adage, "Follow your heart." Your heart is a dangerous entity. Following it will most likely end in disaster. Jeremiah warns us that our *"hearts are deceitful above all things, and desperately sick; who can understand it?"* (Jeremiah 17:9). Your heart is dangerous because it is selfish, strong, and leads you to action. This is why we must actively protect our hearts.

Out of your heart flows the springs of life—it is worth protecting. Your heart is like the command center of the soul, mind, will, emotions, and affections and will determine your direction. Look at what Proverbs 23:7 NKJV tells us, *"For as he thinks in his heart, so is he."*

Thomas

Protecting my heart is a top priority for me. I know that as a man my heart can easily be swayed by what I see. So, one way I protect it is by protecting my eyes. I have made a commitment to God and to Lysandra not to open myself up to any other women by guarding what I look at on my computer, TV, and out in the real world. I don't spend time with any women alone. If I need to meet with a woman, Lysandra comes with me. This is one way that I guard my heart.

Lysandra

Guarding my heart is something I do intentionally. I am careful not to allow male friendships to develop too closely. I never talk to another man on the phone privately, I will not ride in a car alone with another man, I don't go to coffee or out to lunch alone with a man, I don't complain to another man about Thomas or my marriage. These are ways I protect my heart from getting too emotionally connected to a male friend.

Fort Knox

Guard your heart like the gold in Fort Knox. Only those with the highest-level security clearance can enter. Even friendships should be closely vetted before allowing them to penetrate your heart's security. Don't allow friends to get too close if they speak negatively about your spouse. Don't give high clearance to a person who doesn't value marriage and doesn't want yours to succeed. Don't welcome friends to influence your heart if they cause division between you and your spouse. Only those who encourage you to be the spouse God wants you to be should be granted access into your heart's depths.

Your heart is designed for God and for your spouse. Who has your heart? There are many people and things battling for your heart. Your friends, children, career, hobbies, sports teams, money, material items, and your own selfishness all strive to be number one. Put God first, followed by your spouse, and watch everything else fall into place.

Make it Personal:

1. In what ways have you experienced your heart being wicked?

2. Why is it dangerous to follow your heart?

3. What people or things are battling for a high place in your heart?

4. What rules and procedures can you implement to guard your heart from the opposite sex?

5. How can you elevate God and your spouse to a higher level in your heart today?

Day 5: Proverbs Chapter 5

Marriage Goal: Enjoy each other sexually.

"Drink water from your own cistern, flowing water from your own well. 18 Let your fountain be blessed, and rejoice in the wife of your youth, 19 a lovely deer, a graceful doe. Let her breasts fill you at all times with delight; be intoxicated always in her love."

Proverbs 5:15, 18–19

Extreme Intoxication

"Is lust always wrong?" We get asked this question frequently. Our answer is no. Lust is a very strong sexual desire. It's great in marriage to have lust (very strong sexual desire) for your spouse and to be intoxicated with your spouse's body, touch, and kiss. God created sex. He wants you to enjoy your sexual relationship. He created it to be fulfilling. He created you to desire sex, to enjoy the look of the opposite sex, and to be physically attracted to your spouse.

His design is for you to love having sex with your spouse. We're reminded in Proverbs 5 that sex should be enjoyed, but there are boundaries to it. Sex isn't to be something you do with just anyone— only the one whom you are married to. Sex is like fire. When it is in the boundaries of a fireplace it brings warmth, peace, and health. When it has no boundaries it brings destruction, devastation, and pain like a forest fire.

Thomas

Guys, we are not only allowed to look at a naked woman but encouraged to enjoy it! The only boundary here is that the naked woman be your own wife. It is good and natural for you to enjoy your wife's body. Her breasts are the only ones that you are to look at and enjoy. Be delighted with them and never get over her body.

Remember how special she is and how privileged you are to be with her. If you're like me, you know you married up. Don't take her or her physique for granted. Enjoy her, caress her, take your time with her, and remind her how much you love her body. Talk specifically about the parts of her figure that turn you on. Kiss every inch of her body.

Your wife wants to know you desire her. She wants to hear you say it. She wants you to treasure her. She wants you to lust after her. Take time today to show her you delight in her physically.

Lysandra

Ladies, sex is good; sex can be great! Don't be afraid to enjoy it. God is in favor of you having a great time in the bedroom with your husband. He wants you to indulge in your sexual relationship. When you can let loose and have fun in the bedroom, sex is amazing! Let go of any hangups or anxiety and fully give yourself to your husband. He will love it—so will you.

Don't be nervous or uncomfortable about talking about sex or trying new sexual adventures. Don't feel weird expressing a desire for your husband's body. He was made for you. Find those aspects of his body you love and tell him why you love them. He wants to feel desired too.

When you have a good time in the bedroom it makes it that much better for him too. Express your love of sex, and make sure he knows you want it and enjoy it. Take a turn initiating sex. When you do, you will take your sex life to a new level.

Be Thankful

When was the last time you thanked God for sex? God created this extraordinary activity for you and your love. He made it awesome! As a couple, take time to pray and thank God for sex. Take turns thanking God for each other's body. Ask Him to bless your sexual encounters. Commit to God and to each other to reserving sex and lust only for one another.

Make it Personal:

1. What do you love about sex?

2. List three aspects of your spouse's body you lust after and why.

3. Talk about the things your spouse does during sex that you like.

4. Thank God together for sex.

5. Pray together and ask God to bless your sexual experiences.

Day 6: Proverbs Chapter 6

Marriage Goal: Commit to being faithful to one another.

*"Can a man carry fire next to his chest and his clothes not be burned? 28
Or can one walk on hot coals and his feet not be scorched? 32 He who
commits adultery lacks sense; he who does it destroys himself. 33 He will
get wounds and dishonor, and his disgrace will not be wiped away."*

Proverbs 6:27–28, 32–33

You're Hurting Yourself

There is a lie we are all capable of convincing ourselves to believe when
it comes to giving into our lust toward others. You can convince yourself
it won't hurt you. It will be a secret, no one will ever find out, your
spouse won't be hurt, and neither will you. These are lies your flesh tells
you. Don't believe them; don't buy into the deception. You are lying to
yourself.

Verse 27 likens extramarital sex to a fire. If you play with fire, you're
going to get burned. When sex is in the boundaries God created, it's
beautiful, brings warmth, and life. When it's outside of God's
boundaries, it brings destruction, pain, and death. Sex outside of
marriage is outside the God-given boundaries. It is no longer safe and
beautiful—it is dangerous. We are told very clearly who you hurt when
you partake in sex outside of marriage; you hurt yourself. Other people
will inevitably be hurt as well, but ultimately, you're causing yourself
harm.

You will create many broken relationships and feel guilt and shame. You
will ruin your marriage. You will hurt your witness for Jesus. You will
lose respect. You will live with regret. You will devastate your spouse.
You will alienate your children. You will destroy your life.

34

Flirting with Disaster

When you flirt with a person of the opposite sex, you're opening yourself to go down a road leading to serious harm. Affairs don't start with an introduction then straight into bed. Infidelity is a slow process of getting to know someone, getting a little closer, sharing secrets, sharing your hearts, then breaking the physical barrier. After that, it won't take long to end up in the bedroom sharing the most intimate act there is, sex.

If you never start down that road, you won't end up at the end of it. If you realize you are on this path now, turn around—run! As Timothy says in 2 Timothy 2:22, *"Flee youthful passions and pursue righteousness, faith, love, and peace, along with those who call on the Lord with a pure heart."*

Check Your Emotions

Understand that it is unfaithful for you to involve in an emotionally close relationship with a person of the opposite sex. If they are so close that they have the same sway over your heart as your spouse, you are in an emotional affair. The relationship is too close if you have conversations with them you wouldn't have with your spouse. This is dangerous, and you are hurting yourself and your marriage relationship.

It's never too late to turn around. Ask God and your spouse for forgiveness. Build up the trust you have lost. Get counseling for you and your spouse to help with the aftermath. Don't give up; your marriage can still be great. We follow a God of miracles. He has the power to rebuild your relationship and bless you with one better than ever before.

Make it Personal:

1. What lies have you believed about being unfaithful?

2. Share a story of yourself or someone you know being unfaithful and how it hurt them.

3. What rules do you both have in place to ensure you never start down the road to an affair?

4. Is there a relationship with the opposite sex from which you need to step back? If so, who?

5. Take time to ask forgiveness from your spouse for any unfaithfulness.

Day 7: Proverbs Chapter 7

Marriage Goal: Highly value the Word of God.

*"My son, keep my words and treasure up my commandments with you;
2 keep my commandments and live;
keep my teaching as the apple of your eye;"*

Proverbs 7:1–2

What Do You Treasure?

When asked, "What do you treasure?" you probably have many things and people flashing through your mind. Hopefully your spouse was there, maybe your kids, your parents, your car, your house, your dog, your bank account, or some rare edition collectable. There are most likely many things and people who make it on your treasured list. There's nothing wrong with that; however, there is something wrong if these things and people come before God.

Did God or the things of God even make the cut for you? Is God's Word a treasure in your life? You may answer quickly, "I'm a Christian, of course I treasure the Bible!" That's great, placing a high value on the Word of God is essential in a close relationship with God and with your spouse, but how highly do you value God's Word?

The Value Gauge

There is a way to know if something is valuable to you in our present-day culture. The greatest commodity in our culture is time. Time is the gauge. There is only so much time in your day, your week, and your year—you don't get more or less than anyone else. This makes time incredibly valuable. People rush here and there constantly trying to keep up with their responsibilities and obligations. Many people feel like there just isn't enough time.

That's why when someone chooses to use their most precious commodity of time on you, you feel valued. You feel important to them. That's why you've probably heard someone say, "Thanks for giving me some of your time." Giving someone your time shows them that you value them.

You may say you treasure the Word of God but how much time do you dedicate to it daily? Do you enjoy it, meditate on it, study it, or memorize it? There are many followers of Jesus that don't get into the Bible daily and it is considered an afterthought in their lives. They figure, if they have extra time at the end of their day (and aren't too tired), they'll open the Bible.

Here's what one couple said, "We love the Word of God, but life is really busy, and we have a lot to do. There are times when our Bible sits on the shelf gathering dust. By the time we realize that it's been a while since we read or studied it, weeks have passed."

This study through Proverbs is all about wisdom for you as a couple. It would be wise for each of you to read and study the Word daily by yourself. It would be a wise investment in your marriage if you frequently read and study the Word of God together as a couple. As you show your value of God's Word by reading and studying it together frequently, you will watch your relationship with one another deepen in new and beautiful ways. You will see your wisdom increase in your interactions with each other and with everyone else in your life as well.

On the Right Path

The fact that you are taking time daily to study Proverbs together shows that you're on the path to wisdom. You are showing your value of the Bible. You are showing you value your MVP, most valuable person in your life, your forever partner. Remember, you make time for the things and people who are truly important to you. By doing this devotional book on wisdom, the Word of God, and marriage, you are showing what you treasure. May this be just the beginning of you and your spouse prioritizing the Bible together!

Lysandra

I can think of many times and so many Bible study books that Thomas and I started together. We would determine to study the Word together every night and we would do a great job for two or three days. Sometimes we might make it a week, but we always fell away from it eventually. This has been an area of our personal relationship where we have always struggled.

We will never give up on this. We will always attempt to grow in this area and are even now starting a marriage Bible study on the YouVersion Bible app. So, even if you start something and don't finish or are inconsistent, don't give up. Keep recommitting to studying the Word of God together.

Thomas

One thing we do to help each other value God's Word is ask about our personal Bible studies. Lysandra will often ask how my Bible study is going, if I read the Word today, or if God is speaking to me about anything. It's helpful for me to know that she is going to ask me at some point, and I want to have a legitimate answer for her. It encourages me to dive deeper into the Bible.

I will often ask her what she has been studying, and she shares how God speaks to her. This is a way for both of us to turn our minds toward the things of God and helps us to focus on the Scripture's truth, even when we aren't studying the Word in that moment.

Help Each Other

You can be your spouse's biggest cheerleader and encouragement to be in the Word of God. Ask them what they are studying. Ask them what they learned. Ask how consistent they're being in Scripture daily. Share what you are learning and what you are studying. Talk often about the Bible and the truth of the Word. As you do, you will increase your value of God's Word and deepen your relationship with God—and your spouse.

Make it Personal:

1. From one to ten, how much do you value the Word of God?

2. What could you get rid of to make more time for God's Word?

3. Is there anything or anyone who you value more than God?

4. How can you, as a couple, devote more time to the things of God?

5. What can you do to gently encourage your spouse to be faithful to the Word of God?

Day 8: Proverbs Chapter 8

Marriage Goal: Speak as wisdom speaks.

"Hear, for I will speak noble things, and from my lips will come what is right, 7 for my mouth will utter truth; wickedness is an abomination to my lips. 8 All the words of my mouth are righteous; there is nothing twisted or crooked in them."

Proverbs 8:6–8

Wisdom's Words

This passage defines the way wisdom sounds when spoken. Notice the description of wisdom's words: noble, right, truth, no wickedness, righteous, nothing twisted, nothing crooked. This is a helpful checklist for the words we speak to our spouse. Imagine a marriage where both partners use only words of wisdom. Imagine the safety, rest, and comfort of only hearing these kinds of words from your spouse.

It's not that you only hear the happy, fluffy, sweet things. No, you hear truth, but it's done in a loving and righteous way. Righteousness isn't "holier than thou." Righteousness is good, virtuous, morality, justice, and decency. That's the way truth is shared. Wisdom's words are good and excellent.

Lysandra

I pray often for wisdom, especially in my words. I need it because I talk a lot! When I was a little girl, my dad used to say, "Lysandra talks just to hear the sound of her own voice." I always disagreed with this, but his point was valid, I was rarely ever quiet. A high quantity of words can get you in trouble—you have a greater chance of saying something ignorant or hurtful. My words have not always been wisdom's words!

One time, I was frustrated with Thomas for not helping me around the house as much as I thought that he should. I tried hard to control my words and only speak kindly, but as the days passed, my disappointment from yesterday layered with my anger from today became bitterness tomorrow. Eventually, my anger seeped out in passive aggressive words, not wisdom's words.

As Thomas sat on the couch playing a game on his phone, I said, "Well, I guess I'll just clean out the garage by myself like I do everything else by myself. You just keep playing your game."

I'm still embarrassed of my words and attitude. And as you probably already guessed, my passive aggressive words didn't work anyway. They weren't the way to get to my husband's heart or his actions.

Thomas

When she talks that way to me, I have no desire to help her. My natural response is to defend myself and point out her flaws because I feel like I'm being attacked. I also don't really know if there's even a problem. I'm basically clueless until she tells me she's upset.

Lysandra has gained wisdom in her speech over the years. Now, when she wants my help cleaning the garage, she says very directly and kindly, "I need your help cleaning the garage this week. Can you give me a day and time to help me?" I am happy to help her whenever she asks me.

Examine Your Words

What do your words sound like? Do your words sound like wisdom's words or a fool's words? Take a moment to think about every item on this list and examine your words to your spouse. Do you pass the test of wisdom's words? Are your words noble, right, true, without wickedness, righteous, nothing twisted, nothing crooked?

If you are guilty of unwise words, own it. Admit it out loud to your spouse. Apologize for the way you've spoken to them. Ask your spouse to forgive your nasty words. Pray, asking God to give you wisdom's words. Tell your spouse that you are working on this with the power of the Holy Spirit. He has all wisdom and power, and He alone has the power to change those that want to change!

Make it Personal:

1. Write the seven-point checklist describing wisdom's words.

2. With which of these seven items do you struggle most?

3. Describe your view of righteousness in speech.

4. Share a time your words were foolish rather than wise.

5. Write down a prayer for your words to become wisdom's words.

Day 9: Proverbs Chapter 9

Marriage Goal: Accept correction and reproof.

*"Whoever corrects a scoffer gets himself abuse, and he who reproves a
wicked man incurs injury. 8 Do not reprove a scoffer, or he will hate you;
reprove a wise man, and he will love you. 9 Give instruction to a wise
man, and he will be still wiser; teach a righteous man,
and he will increase in learning."*

Proverbs 9:7–9

You Aren't Perfect

Our toxic trait as humans is to deceive ourselves that we're "pretty
good" or even perfect. We believe our way is best, our thinking makes
the most sense, and our perspective is the only one that matters. By our
very nature we are selfish and arrogant. This is why there are many
arguments in marriage. Our pride whispers in our ear, "You're right."

If we don't fight the prideful urge to view ourselves as perfect, we aren't
able to receive correction or advice. This makes us a foolish, wicked
scoffer.

Thomas

In my natural self, I am that guy—the guy you can't tell anything to. God
has worked on me greatly over the last twenty plus years of marriage,
but at the beginning, Lysandra couldn't tell me anything. I wouldn't
listen to her. I thought my way was best basically all the time. The
direction I wanted to take in the car was better than her way. My way
to lead the youth ministry was better than her opinion. My way to
handle our girls' discipline was better than her technique. My way to
interact socially was better than her way.

After years of acting this way, it led to Lysandra believing I didn't respect her. Which wasn't true; I respected her in so many ways. To this day, I believe she is the best human on the planet. I just had so much pride I couldn't admit to being wrong or see that there was more than one way to accomplish something.

Lysandra

After being married for a while, I understood my thoughts and opinions were not being valued and many times not even welcome to be voiced. I decided I wouldn't share my thoughts anymore. What was the point? Thomas was going to do it his own way anyway.

Then, we got lost. We were driving from Foley, Alabama into the country to pick up some kids on the church bus early Sunday morning. Thomas took a wrong turn, and I knew it. Based on previous drives I had learned to keep my mouth shut and not tell him—he would have to figure it out on his own.

After several miles he said, "This doesn't look right." I said, "You're right, you missed your turn back at that four-way stop two miles ago." He got mad and said, "If you knew, why didn't you tell me?" I reminded him what happened the last few times I gave him advice while driving and how he reacted to me. I said, "I've learned not to correct your driving." He was very frustrated, realizing we were now going to be late to the church service we were leading.

I expected him to be mad at me, but to my delight he was mad at himself. He apologized for treating me that way in the past and assured me that in the future he would welcome my advice while driving, and he has ever since.

Wisdom Welcomes Advice

A wise person, not only doesn't get mad when they're confronted with correction or advice, but they even welcome it and are grateful for it. Think in terms of your marriage. Your spouse has a lot to offer you. They know you. They've watched how you interact with people, how you fail and succeed. They know where you've made mistakes or sinned.

They have a unique window into your life and soul that no other human has. They can give you more intelligent advice than anyone else on this earth. Your spouse sees areas you need reproof in more than anyone else in your circle. Give them permission to share their counsel and advice with you. When they do, accept it. Say the words that can be tough to say, "You're right." Tell them thank you, that you needed to hear that. Then make the necessary changes in your plan.

Thomas

I've watched Lysandra over the years. She is strong, intelligent, creative, kind, socially graceful, and wise. Now I go to her with everything. I want her opinion on all my graphic design work, my social interactions, my sermon series plans, my parenting, and my spiritual growth. I welcome and respect everything she has to say. I have given her permission and asked her to share her wisdom with me. I am wise enough now to know I need her advice and counsel.

Lysandra

Thomas has shown me innumerable times that he respects my opinions and has responded well to counsel I've given him. Because of this, I now know that I can share my heart with him, and I invite him to do the same with me.

Beware of how you give advice to your spouse. It must never be in a condescending way, in public, in a spirit of pride, or in anger. This is not wisdom, it's foolish. Correction, counsel, and advice must be given in humility and love, in private at the appropriate time, and with a goal of helping your spouse.

It Benefits You

If you are wise enough to accept and listen to advice, reproof, and correction, you will improve your own quality of life. Your life will be better. You will be smarter. You will have greater business success. You will have deeper relationships. You will be happier. Accepting reproof and advice causes you to be wiser. Being wise makes you a better person. Being a better person helps you become a better spouse. Being a better spouse gives you a better marriage. It all benefits you!

Make it Personal

1. In what areas do you tend to think you know best?

2. In what three areas of life is it hardest for you to hear instruction or correction?

3. Who has permission to give you advice?

4. How do you typically respond to your spouse giving you counsel or advice?

5. List the benefits you get from being humble enough to receive reproof.

Day 10: Proverbs Chapter 10

Marriage Goal: Choose your words carefully.

"When words are many, transgression is not lacking, but whoever restrains his lips is prudent. 20 The tongue of the righteous is choice silver; the heart of the wicked is of little worth. 21 The lips of the righteous feed many, but fools die for lack of sense."

Proverbs 10:19–21

The Quantity of Words

There are times when the best thing you can do for your marriage and for your spouse is to stop talking. We had a friend who would put his foot in his mouth when talking to his wife and then would try to dig himself out of the hole he had dug. It would go from bad to worse. His wife would say, "Stop saying words!" This is good advice we should heed. There are times in marriage when the wisest option is to hold your tongue, because as verse 19 tells us, *"When words are many, transgression is not lacking."*

If you're always speaking, chances are, you're going to say words that aren't beneficial. A plethora of words can become careless or worse, hurtful. When you're speaking to your spouse, think first. Don't talk incessantly. Nonstop words may result in nonstop wreckage.

Lysandra

This is a real challenge for me, basically all the time. I process verbally and think by speaking rather than thinking first. I try words on to see how they fit. If I realize I don't like what I'm saying, I will keep talking to see if that's the truest way I feel or the real way I think. This has been a problem numerous times in my past.

My parents warned me repeatedly that my mouth would one day get me into trouble—they were right. There have been many times where I spoke worthless, careless, and eventually hurtful words. My parents' warning still replays in my mind as I try to turn off the firehose of words that project from my mouth. Slow down, be aware, be wise. Wisdom uses a "less is more" approach, preventing idle, careless, and hurtful words.

The Quality of Words

It's much easier to use quality words if you're thinking carefully about what you say before you speak. When you use fewer words, the chances of using quality words rises substantially. As verse 19 states, *"Whoever restrains his lips is prudent."* This word *prudent* has the idea of sensible, careful, and wise.

Don't you want your words to your spouse to be prudent: sensible, careful, and wise? Don't you want quality words to be shared in your marriage?

The Power of Words

Words hold a great deal of power. The better you know someone, the more weight your words have. In fact, your words have more hold over your spouse than anyone else in this world. This reality places a massive responsibility on your shoulders. We all know, with great power comes great responsibility.

Death and life are in the power of the tongue. No one can hurt you like your spouse can hurt you. No one can hurt your spouse like you can hurt them; you have the potential to bring death to their spirit. The most admirable marriage is the one where both spouses are completely and totally authentic and vulnerable with one another. This creates a close and intimate relationship, unmatched by any other. Sounds great, right? It is; however, because you know your spouse better than anyone, you have more power to speak death to their soul too.

Thomas

I know Lysandra's deepest insecurities. I know what she's afraid of and what she doesn't like about herself. I could easily destroy her with the words that I say. In a split second I could wound her so deeply she would not heal for a long time, if ever. With this kind of power comes great responsibility. I have a responsibility to control my words and protect her from the damage my words could inflict.

The Positive Power of Words

No one has the power to speak death to your spouse's soul like you. Thankfully, the reverse is also true. Your words can convey encouragement, joy, positivity, and health in your spouse's spirit. What a lovely gift we can bless each other with!

Your words are valuable to your spouse, not because of their quantity but because of their quality. Remember what verse 20 says, *"The tongue of the righteous is choice silver."* If your words are wise and righteous, they are valuable, like the most expensive and refined silver. They are words to be desired and sought after. They will breathe life into your marriage relationship. It's time we choose our words carefully.

Make it Personal

1. Describe the way you process thoughts, verbally or internally.

2. In what situations do you need to think more carefully before you speak?

3. What words have your spouse spoke in the past that have crushed your spirit?

4. What does the term "quality words" mean to you?

5. Speak ten words of life to your spouse today.

Day 11: Proverbs Chapter 11

Marriage Goal: Look for the good in one another.

"Whoever diligently seeks good seeks favor,
but evil comes to him who searches for it."

Proverbs 11:27

You Find What You're Looking For.

Have you ever noticed that when you buy a new car, you begin to see that same car everywhere? As you're leaving the grocery store looking for your white SUV, it seems like there are one hundred white SUVs in the parking lot. You may even accidentally climb into the wrong one! You see every white SUV because you are looking for a white SUV. You don't notice the twenty black sedans in that same parking lot because you're not looking for a black sedan. This is also true with positivity or negativity in your spouse.

Abraham Lincoln said, "Those who look for the bad in people will surely find it." Think of your spouse's annoying habit. Think of that thing they do that drives you crazy. Think of that phrase they say that always makes you mad. Think of the chore that they often leave undone. If you focus on the bad and actively look for it, you will notice it every time. It's like expecting them to fail and then when they do, acting surprised or angry about it. Whatever you look for in your spouse is what you will find.

Search for Positivity

Now that you've thought of all your spouse's negative qualities, consider their positive qualities. The best way to change the way you see your spouse is to search for positivity in them. Trust us, it's there; you just have to look for it. Searching for positivity in your spouse is wisdom.

Proverbs 11:27 says, *"Whoever diligently seeks good seeks favor, but evil comes to him who searches for it."*

It's like looking for your car in the grocery store parking lot. When you look for it, you will eventually find it, and you will end up noticing many similar ones. Start the search for positivity by looking for one good thing your spouse does regularly. For example, goes to work, comes home every night and cooks, puts laundry in the hamper, gives hugs, spends time with the kids, helps with homework, takes the dogs out, etc. Think about every good thing they do.

As you look for the good things, you will notice other good things they do.

Lysandra

Toward the beginning of our marriage, I struggled to see all the good in Thomas. There were many times I thought, "He's so mean!" My thoughts spiraled to a lot more negative ones about him. I thought, "He's lazy, he's not as spiritually focused as I thought he would be, he doesn't care about me ..." From here, it was easy to notice all the times I felt he was mean to me. It became second nature for me to see the other negative things I thought about him. I didn't have to work at it— at all. His faults became blaringly obvious to me nearly all the time.

I knew something had to change. I was slowly becoming a wife who didn't like her husband. I started trying to look for good things he did. I would rehearse them in my mind when he did something I didn't like. If he was mean, or what I considered mean, I would remind myself of something kind he had done for me. I looked for times he worked hard. I realized there was great value in him simply going to work every day. I tried to appreciate the times he would pray and value that he was faithful to go to church at every opportunity. I filed it away in my mind when he carried my heavy bag, realizing he did care about me. I began to see more and more positive actions.

I began to like my husband again. When I looked for the bad, I found it easily; when I looked for the good it was there, just not as obvious. It takes more effort to find the good than the bad in your spouse, but it is there.

The Search Continues

Next, in your search for positivity in your spouse, think about every good thing they say. Notice the times they say thank you. Be aware of how often they say I love you or use positive words with your children. Don't forget their conversations with you, and how they share their thoughts and feelings. These are good words too. You want that open communication in a relationship. Think about the times they say good morning or goodbye to you in kind, friendly ways; these count as good words they say.

Now, think of their positive character traits. This is not what they say or do but who they are. Here are a few examples to get you started: courageous, creative, loyal, ambitious, confident, humorous, compassionate, kind, forgiving, clever, fair, honest, gentle, persistent, cheerful, reliable. If you're still struggling to identify your spouse's positive character traits, here are a few questions to help you.

- Do they go to work daily? Then they are a hard worker.
- Are they honest about work, hours, etc.? Then they are honest.
- Do they read their Bible and pray? They are spiritual.
- Do they play with the kids? Then they are energetic, selfless, and loving.

Now that you have thought of good actions they do, good words they say, and good character traits, over the next week, look for these things. You are guaranteed to see positivity far more often than you realized. When you look for the good, you will find it.

Make it Personal:

1. Make a list of all the good things your spouse does.

2. Make a list of all the good things your spouse says.

3. Make a list of all your spouse's positive character traits.

4. Verbally express gratitude for the items on your lists.

5. Share the ways you plan to look for positivity in your spouse this week.

Day 12: Proverbs Chapter 12

Marriage Goal: Bring one another healing with words.

"There is one whose rash words are like sword thrusts, but the tongue of the wise brings healing. 25 Anxiety in a man's heart weighs him down, but a good word makes him glad."

Proverbs 12:18, 25

Deep Wounds in Seconds

You've probably heard the adage, "Sticks and stones will break my bones, but words will never hurt me." But the truth is, words can and often do hurt us. Think of a time someone said hurtful words to you in your childhood. A memory just flashed into your mind, right? Words cut deep wounds in seconds but, years and years later, you can still remember them. Hopefully by now they are memories without shame and hurt, but that isn't always the case. Words from childhood can haunt you for life. The warning of Proverbs 12:18 ring true, *"There is one whose rash words are like sword thrusts."*

There are some things we simply can't get over quickly—they're too deep to disappear into thin air. These wounds could be from childhood, past relationships, parents, teachers, or trusted friends. Healing from significant wounds takes a significant amount of time.

Be gentle with your spouse as you sit with them and the pain they are trying to let go of. Give them grace. Understand that healing is a process not an event. Patiently be there for them. Love them unconditionally. Walk with them in their journey to healing.

Assist in Their Healing

As you choose wise words, remember the last part of Proverbs 12:18 that you can help them heal, *"... the tongue of the wise brings healing."*

Your carefully chosen words can beautifully bind up their wounds as a doctor would treat a physical laceration. What a beautiful picture!

If your spouse was severely wounded in a car accident and you had the tools and knowledge to treat their physical wound, you would do it without hesitation. Yet, we can be so stingy with healing words. We can become callous and unfeeling toward the one we are called to love the most in our world. We feel like they've held onto the hurt long enough. We think they should be "over it" by now. We withhold the good from them when it is in our power to give it.

Thomas

Lysandra has struggled with physical insecurities since she was a very young teenager. Words spoken at inopportune times in her adolescence paired with sexual abuse created a deep wound that wouldn't heal overnight. My goal from the beginning of our relationship was to assist her in her healing journey. I knew she needed to hear words of health frequently to combat the unhealthy words she heard almost constantly in her mind.

It wasn't always easy. She could not receive positive words from me early on. Any words of truth and health I spoke were met with opposition or arguments. I was repeatedly accused of lying to her. There were many times my words of life were met with tears. I was tempted many times to give up. Thankfully God gave me the wisdom to understand this was all part of her long journey toward emotional healing. I understood that I didn't get to choose how long healing would take, but I could choose if I wanted to assist in the process. She is better now but some things still trigger her and when they do, I'm ready to speak life to my wife.

Till Death Do Us Part

You vowed "till death do us part" to your spouse. Never give up on them. Don't get weary of speaking those important words of life to them. Your spouse needs you; they need your words of wisdom and positivity. It can take between five to seven positive words to outweigh one negative. This means if we're going to make a difference in our spouse's emotional health, we need to speak positivity to them frequently. It's time to take this responsibility seriously—we need to up our game. Proverbs 12:25 challenges us, *"A good word makes him glad."* Be the reason your spouse is glad today.

Make it Personal:

1. Share something hurtful someone said to you in your childhood.

2. Based on what your spouse just shared, list five positive things about them within that topic.

3. Take a moment to apologize for not being patient as your spouse heals from a past emotional wound if needed.

4. As you reflect on the vows from your wedding day, re-promise a few to your love.

5. In what area do you need to speak life more frequently into your spouse?

Day 13: Proverbs Chapter 13

Marriage Goal: Spend time with other godly couples.

"Whoever walks with the wise becomes wise,
but the companion of fools will suffer harm."

Proverbs 13:20

You Are What You Eat

We've all heard it since we were children, "You are what you eat." There's some wisdom to that statement, what we eat will eventually catch up with us, it's true. A more piercing statement would be "You are who you hang out with." We often think of this as important for teenagers, which is true, but it applies to each of us at all of life's stages. It's an important truth for married couples as we are significantly influenced by those with whom we spend the most time.

As you and your spouse spend time with other couples, consider the effect they will have on you.

- Are you spending time with a couple who talks negatively about one another?
- Do your couple friends have a godly, healthy marriage?
- Would God be pleased if you began to act more like your go-to couple?
- Are your closest friends drawing you and your spouse toward Jesus or away from Him?

Peer pressure is alive and well—it's not just for adolescents. There is data that suggests a couple is more likely to get a divorce if they spend a significant amount of time with other divorcees. According to Forbes Advisor, "Having friends who are divorced increases your risk of divorce. The marital stability within a couple's social network also plays a role in whether their union lasts. Couples who have friends who divorce have a 75 percent increase in the risk of their marriage ending. Even couples with two degrees of separation from divorce still have a 33 percent greater risk. Because of this link, some sociologists believe divorce is a social contagion."[1]

Positive Peer Pressure

Usually, this principle of becoming like those you spend time with is used to warn people against spending too much time with the wrong element. Remember that the reverse is also true. Spending time with those who are wise will influence you in the way of wisdom just as Proverbs 13:20 reads, *"Whoever walks with the wise becomes wise."*

Surround yourselves with people who encourage you to invest in your marital relationship. Make time in your schedule for couples that draw you closer to God. Spend time with couples who love and respect one another. Seek out couples who pursue wisdom.

Lysandra

When our four daughters were young, we never went on double dates. We were so starved for one-on-one time that we didn't want to share it with another couple. We made an exception to our rule one time and really regretted it.

We got the babysitter and met the other couple at a local restaurant. When we got there, they were waiting for us in a booth; it was immediately evident that the two were fighting. Throughout dinner they complained and berated one another under the poor disguise of sarcasm and awkward laughter. The whole evening was a disaster. We swore to one another we wouldn't waste another date night on a double date.

Thomas

We broke our rule several years later when another nice couple invited us to dinner. We reluctantly went. They were kind to one another. They spoke about the other in respectful and positive ways. We shared our funny stories. We laughed so hard we cried—it was a breath of fresh air! We walked away from that night valuing each other even more than we did before. That was when we understood this principle more clearly than ever. Even as married couples, it matters with whom you spend your time. They will affect you and your marriage relationship.

Seek Them Out

Remember those verses in the earlier chapters in Proverbs about seeking and searching for wisdom? You and your spouse can seek wise couples as well. They are out there. Look for them. Look for couples who speak kindly about one another, even in the absence of the other. Watch for couples who are following Jesus closely. Seek out couples who go the extra mile to help one another and others.

When you spot them, invite them to your home for a meal. Suggest a double date out to your favorite restaurant. Schedule a joint picnic with both of your families at a local park. Find ways to spend time with them and learn from them. If you want to be influenced by wise couples, you must spend time in their presence.

Make it Personal:

1. Describe a time when you were influenced by peer pressure.

2. Name a couple with whom you know you should not spend more time.

3. Name a couple with whom you feel you should spend more time.

4. Share some ideas of ways you will plan to develop your friendship with that couple.

5. List three ways you can be a good influence on another couple.

Day 14: Proverbs Chapter 14

Marriage Goal: Controlling your tempers.

"A man of quick temper acts foolishly, and a man of evil devices is hated. 29 "Whoever is slow to anger has great understanding, but he who has a hasty temper exalts folly."

Proverbs 14:17, 29

Angry Opportunities

The opportunities in marriage to lose your temper are limitless and never ending. It is amazing how quickly your spouse can make you angry.

When your spouse leaves their dirty socks on the floor, when they forget your anniversary, when they choose work rather than time with you, or when they place the empty milk jug back in the refrigerator, there's an opportunity to let your temper flare.

If you allow your temper to operate without restraint, it can destroy your marriage.

Thomas

For most of my life, I have had a real problem with my temper—it almost prevented my marrying Lysandra. Our wedding was only two weeks away, and we were on our way from Cedar Rapids to Walker, Iowa. I was driving Lysandra's little Toyota Camry on a deserted country road in Iowa. Suddenly, we heard a loud pop, and the car was difficult to keep on the road. We had a flat tire.

I pulled over to the shoulder and shifted the car into park. I was angry—so angry! I started hitting the dashboard, yelling, and cussing up a storm. I let my anger loose and it created what can only be described as an adult temper tantrum. It was ugly. Lysandra sat still and quiet in the passenger seat doing her best not to make eye contact with me. I got out and began to change the tire. It didn't take long, and we were back on the road again. When we got to her parents' house, Lysandra said she didn't want to get out of the car. We sat in the driveway as she poured out her heart to me through her tears.

She explained that she wasn't afraid to call off the wedding and tell all the guests that it was off. She was afraid to marry someone with an unruly temper. She said words that stuck with me forever, "One day, you're going to stop hitting the dashboard and you're going to hit me. I won't marry you if your temper is out of control. I love you, but I won't ruin my life to marry you."

This was the exact wakeup call I needed. I promised her I would change. I promised that I would work on my quick temper. From that moment on, I tried so hard to control my temper. I failed sometimes, and I still do occasionally, but I'm growing. My temper is not nearly as volatile as it once was. Now, it is a very rare occasion for me to get uncontrollably angry.

My temper almost ruined my marriage before I even had a chance to say, "I do."

Lysandra

I get angry sometimes, but I never really struggled with losing my temper ... until recently that is. It was about four months ago that I caught myself losing my temper over the stupidest things. I would drop my keys or stub my toe and get so mad I would throw something or kick something. I was indulging in my anger.

The Lord spoke to me about this one day after I threw an adult temper tantrum in front of my teenage daughters. They quietly stood by in disbelief. I was certainly acting foolishly just as Proverbs said, *"A man of quick temper acts foolishly, and a man of evil devices is hated."* My heart was broken before the Lord. I apologized to my children and to God. I asked for forgiveness and made a commitment to work on this new flaw in my character. I really prayed about it that day.

Only twenty-four hours later, I found old rotten bacon and feta cheese in my trunk that one of my girls had forgotten to bring inside after grocery shopping. I picked it up and threw it back down in the trunk. I then looked at my daughter and said, "Didn't I say just yesterday that I wasn't going to do this anymore?" I sighed, rolled my eyes and we both had a good laugh. Since then, that's the last time I let my temper get out of control.

My quick temper will destroy my family if I let it, and so will yours.

The Flip Side

There are two sides to every story. If your temper is out of control, you will act foolishly, say hurtful words, and ruin relationships, but there is more to this, and we find it on the flip side. The other side is that when you are slow to anger and controlled in your behavior, you have great understanding; you are wise, just as Proverbs 14:29 says, *"Whoever is slow to anger has great understanding."*

The foolishness that exists when your temper goes wild has the equal and opposite impact of the wisdom that exists when you control your anger and choose to do right. Imagine a life where you rarely, if ever, have to apologize for saying something you shouldn't have. Consider the peace in your home when everyone is slow to anger and quick to forgive. Imagine a marriage where neither partner has to be afraid of an angry outburst or temper tantrum. This is a life of safety, peace, and rest. With wisdom, you can have this kind of life.

Make it Personal:

1. What is something that your spouse does that makes you angry?

2. How have you responded to them in the past?

3. Describe a time you threw an adult temper tantrum.

4. What changes will you make to respond in love in the future?

5. What are some benefits of having your temper under control?

Day 15: Proverbs Chapter 15

Marriage Goal: Speak life to one another.

"A soft answer turns away wrath, but a harsh word stirs up anger. 2 The tongue of the wise commends knowledge, but the mouths of fools pour out folly. 4 A gentle tongue is a tree of life, but perverseness in it breaks the spirit."

Proverbs 15:1–2, 4

Cause and Effect

The words you speak to your spouse will most assuredly have a consequence; they are powerful in your spouse's life and will affect your marriage relationship. Every action causes an effect. Harsh words build anger in your spouse. Foolish words create problems. Perverse words crush a spirit. You cannot believe the lie that what you say to your spouse doesn't matter—it does.

When a word is said, it no longer belongs to you. You thought it in your mind, spoke it out of your mouth, and now it lives in the mind of the receiver who deals with the effects of it. You cannot get those words back or modify them; they now belong to your spouse. This is why the things we say are so significant.

If you tell your spouse that they are worthless, those words are in their mind affecting their soul forever. If you use harmful words, such as ugly, fat, unattractive, or gross, those words will break their spirit. If you call them stupid, useless, or pointless, those words will bring death. Your words greatly influence your spouse. Your words affect your spouse forever.

Life Giver

You have so much power every day to positively affect your spouse and change their life forever in a positive way. The things you say can bring them life—your words can change how they view themselves, what they believe they are capable of, and how they feel. That's a great deal of power! Commit today to use it for good.

Here are some examples of words of life your spouse should hear you say regularly.

- I love you.
- I appreciate what you do.
- I'm glad I married you.
- You are making a difference.
- You are beautiful/handsome.
- I love that I wake up next to you every day.
- You work hard.
- I'm thankful you have good character.
- I'm blessed to be your partner.
- I'm so happy that I get to spend forever with you.
- You are a great mom/dad.
- I love the way you think.
- You are an awesome person.
- You're funny.
- You're clever.
- You're gifted.
- You're so talented.
- You're fun.
- You're funny.
- You're good at what you do.
- You're the one I want to spend time with.

Now, use this list as a starting point for you and your spouse to speak words of life and transform your marriage.

Lysandra

I can't think of a time when Thomas spoke harsh words to me. He is very careful of the things he says. He is an intense guy, but he chooses to use gentle words with me. My Facebook was recently hacked, and it was stolen. I was so angry thinking of some stranger trying to swindle my friends and acquaintances out of money using my name. I was powerless, frustrated, and upset.

We happened to be leaving on vacation the morning that it was stolen. I was sitting on my closet floor quietly packing the last few items in my suitcase. Thomas came in, bent over, and put his hands on my arms and spoke words of life to my spirit.

"I'm so sorry this happened to you. I know how frustrated you are, I'm frustrated too. This isn't right. I will keep trying to get it back for you. I love you," he said.

It was so simple and brief, yet it brought my spirit life. I felt a breath of fresh air inside where there was turmoil and irritation. His words were just what I needed to hear in that moment.

Thomas

I'm thankful for my wife's words of life. There have been times when work was so difficult and overwhelming that I seriously considered quitting. No matter who you are or what position you hold, work can be discouraging and crushing. I'm a Pastor, and it isn't always easy. I remember one week when it felt like everything I strived to accomplish was failing. It seemed that everyone I was ministering to was rejecting my advice, help, and leading.

I was in a particularly dark place when Lysandra walked into our room and said, "I know it's hard but look at those you've impacted in just a few short years. Think about where we were as a church and how far we've come." Then she proceeded to list all the people who had made progress in their faith journey. She talked about how the work I was doing was important and she even said words I rarely hear, "You're a good pastor."

She had no idea how she breathed life into me that day. Her words were soft, gentle, and wise. She had the power to break my spirit or act as a tree of life. Because she chose life, I didn't quit. I'm so thankful for a wife who uses her words to bring me life.

Transform Moments

It's not about grand gestures or eloquent speeches. It's the daily, miniscule interactions you have with your spouse. Every seemingly insignificant moment is an opportunity for you to change your spouse's spirit. It's the moments you say goodbye before work, the times you see your spouse frustrated, the instances you catch them out of the corner of your eye looking sad. It's the good morning moments every single day. It's the apparently inconsequential flashes of time where you choose to take an interaction that could be damaging or meaningless and transform it into a tree of life for your spouse.

Make it Personal:

1. Give examples of harsh, foolish, or perverse things one could say to a spouse.

2. Give examples of soft, wise, or gentle words one could say to a spouse.

3. Are there words you have said to your spouse for which you need to apologize?

4. Share a time when your spouse spoke words of life into you.

5. Make a commitment to one another to speak only wise, gentle words of life in your marriage.

Day 16: Proverbs Chapter 16

Marriage Goal: Develop a peaceful home.

"When a man's ways please the Lord,
he makes even his enemies to be at peace with him."

Proverbs 16:7

Friend or Foe

You planned a wedding for months, booked the honeymoon, and dreamed of everything your marriage would be. Then you walked down the aisle and said, "I do." Your marriage began. It's puzzling how after the honeymoon phase wears off, this best friend who you were thrilled to spend forever with can somehow feel like your enemy.

This spouse God gave you is supposed to be your biggest fan, your partner, and your closest confidant. Yet, after years of the marriage grind, hurt, unresolved conflict, and the business of life, your friend can at times feel like your enemy.

Whether friend or foe, or somewhere in between, strive to be at peace with your spouse.

Peace doesn't always come easy. Look at the history books. Wars must progress quite severely to reach a peace treaty. Once the strongest opponent has fought their hardest, used every tactic, and proven they have the military might and arsenal to destroy the other, the enemy cowers, eventually surrenders, and signs the peace treaty.

Can we skip the marital warfare and achieve peace without unnecessary blood shed? The answer is yes. Proverbs gives us the strategic peace plan. Achieving peace isn't about battle plans or attack strategies. Focus on pleasing the Lord. When you please Him, you find peace with your spouse, whether they feel like a friend or foe. Peace is about pursuing God and His kingdom, and then watching everything else in your life fall into place. Notice the promise that Jesus gives in Matthew 6:33, *"But seek first the Kingdom of God and His righteousness, and all these things will be added to you."*

When you and your spouse are living a life of pleasing the Lord you will have peace in your home.

Pleasing God

R.C. Sproul said it this way, "There is no way of learning more accurately or more quickly about what is pleasing to God, than studying the law of God."[2]

Here are ways that Scripture tells us we can please the Lord:

- Hebrew 11:6 tells us we must live by faith if we are to please God, *"And without faith it is impossible to please him, for whoever would draw near to God must believe that he exists and that he rewards those who seek him."*
- In Galatians 1:10, we learn that we are to be servants of Christ, *"For am I now seeking the approval of man, or of God? Or am I trying to please man? If I were still trying to please man, I would not be a servant of Christ."*
- Psalm 147:10–11 tells us to fear God and hope in His love, *"His delight is not in the strength of the horse, nor his pleasure in the legs of a man, 11 but the Lord takes pleasure in those who fear him, in those who hope in his steadfast love."*
- According to Hebrews 13:15–16, we can please God with our praise, *"Through him then let us continually offer up a sacrifice of praise to God, that is, the fruit of lips that acknowledge his name. 16 Do not neglect to do good and to share what you have, for such sacrifices are pleasing to God."*

These are a few of the ways that we can live lives that are pleasing to Him.

MVP

Your home and your marriage were never meant to be a war zone. God didn't create marriage so you would always have someone with which to fight. Your spouse is not your enemy; they are your greatest asset and teammate. If you have been viewing your spouse as an enemy or opponent, we challenge you to change your perception of them. It's time to see them as your greatest gift from God and your MVP (most valuable person).

You, most likely, don't have a picture-perfect marriage—those don't really exist. But peaceful, content marriages do exist, and they happen when two people team up and seek to please God, leaving the rest to Him. If you are living your life to please God, then you experience how great it is to enjoy peace in your home and in your marriage.

Lysandra

I think one of the very best things about following God wholeheartedly is the peace that goes with this close relationship. It is absolutely beautiful to experience harmony in life and peace in a marriage relationship.

This is important to me because I despise conflict. When Thomas and I fight, or even when something's merely a little off, I just hate it. I can't fully rest or relax. I'm uncomfortable until the issue is cleared up and we're close again. I'm longing for peace until then. When peace returns, due to proper communication and appropriate conflict resolution, I feel a tangible weight lifted, both physically and emotionally. This is why the promise in Proverbs 16:7 is so precious to me, *"When a man's ways please the Lord, he makes even his enemies to be at peace with him."*

Thomas

I don't mind conflict, and it doesn't irritate me nearly as much as Lysandra to be at odds for a short amount of time. However, for her sake, I strive for peace as quickly as possible in our relationship. I know she needs it more than I do. Maybe you're like me and it's not bothersome to lose a little peace at home. If that's the case, consider your spouse's need for peace.

Make it your top priority to please the Lord in all you think, say, and do. This will help you foster peace, not only for yourself, but more importantly for your spouse.

Live to Please

You are living your life to please someone. Most of us naturally live to please ourselves; sometimes we work hard to please others. Wisdom tells us to live to please God. Are you living for the applause of men or of nail-scarred hands? Is your life about your own pleasure or about God's glory? Choose today to live to please God above all else.

Make it Personal:

1. How did marriage surprise you once the honeymoon stage was over?

2. Describe a time when you viewed your spouse as your enemy or opponent.

3. In what ways do you need to better seek to please the Lord?

4. Who in your marriage is most uncomfortable with conflict?

5. List three ways that make your spouse your MVP.

Day 17: Proverbs Chapter 17

Marriage Goal: Always cultivate a loving friendship.

"A friend loves at all times, and a brother is born for adversity."

Proverbs 17:17

So Cliché

"I married my best friend." You hear it all the time. If you don't buy into these romanticized ideas, hearing these phrases can make you sick. But, if you really did marry your friend and you developed the relationship, your spouse can turn into your best friend and life can be awesome! Being married to your best friend is extraordinary. It is a blessing many don't have, so, if you are married to your best friend, thank God for that.

If you can't honestly say that you married your best friend, don't lose hope. Here are some simple ways you can begin to develop your friendship today.

Be Kind

It seems the person we are toughest on is our own spouse. We believe they'll never leave us, so we treat them worse than anyone else in our world. Don't forget to be kind; no one likes a friend who is rude. Think about the way you talk to them and treat them. Would you want to be your own friend? Use manners and be polite. Speak in tones of love and kindness.

Be Fun

Having fun is a choice. Choose to enjoy spending time with your spouse. Laugh with them. Make jokes. Enjoy activities. Be lighthearted. Don't always be a drag. Be the one they enjoy being around. Remember to consider that what is fun to them may be different than what is fun to you. Fun in friendship requires give and take.

Be Honest

Tell them the truth about what you think and how you feel—but speak that truth in love. Don't forget the first rule of friendship, be kind. It is possible to do both at the same time. Being authentic is something you only do with the highest-level security clearance friend. Allow that person to be your spouse. Be honest about who you are.

Be Loyal

Your spouse should be able to trust you wholeheartedly. They should never wonder if you'll be there for them. They should never worry that you will share their inmost personal thoughts, feelings, or insecurities with others. They should never feel anxious that you may be unfaithful. Their heart should safely trust in your complete loyalty. A true friend is loyal and trustworthy.

Be Encouraging

Don't always be that negative voice. Be your spouse's loudest cheerleader. Your spouse needs to hear positive and genuine affirmations from you frequently. Be the one who repeatedly speaks life to your partner. No one wants to be close friends with a consistently negative person. Don't be discouraging; be uplifting.

Be Generous

We can become so stingy with our best friend and spouse. We can get this feeling of entitlement in marriage where we feel like they owe us, and we deserve whatever we want or need from them—whenever we want or need it. Don't be the friend who is always taking; be a friend who is always giving. Be generous with time, love, gifts, gratefulness, space, money, sex, and thoughtfulness.

When Life Gets Hard

As you work to develop your relationship, you will have, not only an awesome marriage, but a terrific friendship—better than any friendship you could ever imagine. When life's challenges rain down, and they will be tough, you will have the most amazing partner who will face them with you.

Life gets real. Tragedy comes, loss happens, things fall apart, and financial difficulties occur. There will be extremely difficult seasons in your life. It's comforting to know you're not in it alone. Your best friend is walking with you through it.

Lysandra

I often look at Thomas and say, "I'm glad we're in this together." Certain days can be difficult, but I know as long as God gives us both breath, we face this life together as a team—a team of best friends. He's always got my back, and I've got his. We succeed together, and we fail together. We walk this journey together, and it's remarkable.

Thomas

Lysandra is my best friend. She brings me joy and laughter, and there's no one else in the world I'd rather spend time or face trials with. This friendship we enjoy didn't just happen. We have invested in each other for years and worked on developing our friendship, and we continue to invest in and develop it. We spend time together and schedule times to have fun with each other. This effort has created a friendship to last and an unbreakable bond.

Not Too Late

You can start today to develop your friendship with your spouse. It's not too late for you two. Maybe this wasn't a priority early on; that doesn't mean you can't have an amazing friendship starting right now. Schedule a date on your calendar; call it a friendship development day. Do something fun that each of you will enjoy. Laugh together, enjoy yourselves, and talk about something real. Investing in your marital friendship will grant you great gain.

Make it Personal:

1. When did your friendship begin?

2. What way do you need to invest in your friendship? Kindness, fun, honesty, loyalty, encouragement, generosity?

3. How have you faced difficult seasons together?

4. Tell your spouse how their friendship has made a difference in your life.

5. Schedule your friendship development day right now.

Day 18: Proverbs Chapter 18

Marriage Goal: Seek to understand one another.

"A fool takes no pleasure in understanding, but only in expressing his opinion. 13 If one gives an answer before he hears, it is his folly and shame."

Proverbs 18:2, 13

Why Are You Such a Jerk?

We know you've thought this about your spouse at some point in your relationship (or something similar). You married a human person who is selfish. You are this same kind of person. We are each the hero of our own story. You think everything, every moment, is about you—so does your spouse. Because of this, there are going to be times when you just feel like you married the "world's biggest jerk".

You come at every interaction from your own perspective, which is your reality. Meanwhile your spouse does the same. This leads to not understanding where they're coming from, and you both seem mean to one another. This can cause you to wonder, "Why is my spouse such a jerk?"

A Little Understanding Goes Far

When you seek to understand your spouse, it makes every interaction easier. When you understand where your spouse is coming from, it's easier to have sympathy, empathy, and patience. There is wisdom in, not just understanding where they come from but also understanding who they are.

Lysandra

I pretty much thought Thomas was a jerk every morning for the first fifteen years of our marriage. I wake up every morning with chipper, top-level, super energy. I am bubbly, happy, and animated from the moment I open my eyes. If you're not a morning person, you hate me right now—I know! I used to turn to Thomas first thing in the morning and give him a bright hello and start talking his ear off about our schedule, how great life is, and the weird dreams I had the night before. He was always unresponsive and cranky. It made me so frustrated because I didn't understand him.

Finally, after fifteen years, we came to an understanding that has helped our relationship in a monumental way. We were on a church camping trip, and we got out of our tent at daybreak. We began to walk to the bathrooms together. I was chattering away incessantly like I do. He was looking cranky like he does. Then, he said the words that changed our marriage, "I need like twenty minutes of quiet in the morning to wake up before I can interact. I'm not a morning person. Can you please help me out and just give me twenty minutes before you talk to me each morning?"

I was so happy to gain this new understanding. He's not just a jerk, he's a night person. All I needed was some understanding so I could be sensitive to how he feels in the morning. Since that camping trip, I am quiet in the mornings. I give Thomas a morning kiss and softly tell him I love him. Then I just lay with him and rub his back. Our relationship has improved greatly! It's incredible what a little understanding can do for a marriage.

Opinions Don't Always Need to be Shared

Our perspective is our reality. Our own opinion just makes the most sense—to us. Just because you have a strong opinion, doesn't mean you must share it every time. It's okay to be quiet sometimes and listen to the other person. It is foolish to always be preparing to debate your own opinion rather than truly listening to the other person and seeking to fully understand them.

Your spouse has good ideas and logical opinions. They have so much to offer; take time to listen to them. Hear them out. While they're talking, actually listen with the goal of gaining a comprehensive understanding of their feelings, thoughts, and perspective. This is wisdom.

Thomas

Lysandra arrived home from working for ten hours straight, came up to my office and slammed the door. "I'm so frustrated with these kids! I told them to do dishes before I got home. The sink is full of dishes, and I can't wash any of my brushes. They're all out there watching TV! No one in this house cares about anyone but themselves!"

This wasn't what I was expecting when my sweet wife came home. It felt like my wife was coming at me. She didn't even say hi, let alone a kiss and hug hello. I was working when interrupted by her coming in angrily venting to me. It's not what I wanted after a long day of work myself; however, I gave my wife grace because I understood how exhausted she was. I understand that her job is physical, and she pushes herself to her limits. When my wife comes home, she wants a shower and to eat a snack in bed. I know my wife. I knew how she was feeling because I understand my Love.

She came at me in anger. My instinct is to tell her, "Chill out, you're not mad at me so stop yelling at me! I didn't leave the dishes in the sink! And I've been working all day too, maybe you could at least say hi before you lay into me?" Understanding where she was coming from helped me to not retaliate in anger. It helped me to know just be quiet and listen. She needed to vent to me; I know that because I understand her. I knew she wanted me to go out there and make our kids get up and do the dishes. Hear your spouse out and seek to understand them, it will greatly benefit your relationship.

Normalize Understanding

Make a commitment today to seek to understand your spouse rather than express your opinion and convince them you're right. Make it the norm in your relationship to understand one another's perspective, opinions, and feelings. Make it second nature to understand who they are. Understanding is the norm in a wise marriage.

Make it Personal:

1. Share a time you thought your spouse was a jerk.

2. How can you understand their side of things now looking back?

3. When did understanding your spouse help you to respond correctly?

4. How can you work on not always sharing your opinion?

5. What will you do to understand your spouse better today?

Day 19: Proverbs Chapter 19

Marriage Goal: Let go of petty offenses.

*"Good sense makes one slow to anger,
and it is his glory to overlook an offense."*

Proverbs 19:11

Grace is Divine

Alexander Pope wrote in the 1700s, "To err is human, to forgive divine." You and your spouse will make mistakes and offend each other repeatedly during your marriage. This is normal humanity. Forgiving those mistakes and offenses is divine or supernatural and from the power of God. It's not natural for to forgive. In fact, it's very difficult for you to forgive, especially your spouse. Wounds from someone so close cut deeply.

We see this idea of overlooking offenses in Proverbs 19. It takes wisdom and grace from God. Grace is something we don't deserve and receive from God every day and night. He showers us with good even though we are undeserving. He gives grace because of who He is; it is an intrinsic part of His character.

As a Christian, married couple, our goal is to become more like Jesus daily. This means offering this kind of divine grace to our spouse regularly.

Thomas

Recently, there was an occasion for me to forgive Lysandra. I had been working at my desk all day when I received a text from her offering to bring me Culvers. She and her parents were running errands and were going to Culvers for dinner. I texted Lysandra my order, and I was looking forward to comfort food as I finished up my work for the day.

About an hour later, Lysandra walked into my office empty handed, kissed me hello, and went about her business. I asked where my dinner was. Her eyes got huge, and her face instantly looked flushed. I knew immediately what had happened. She forgot my dinner. I was disappointed and angry.

She apologized trying to defend her forgetfulness. She offered to go back and get me any food from any restaurant I wanted. I didn't have time before my next appointment for that. The opportunity had passed; it was too late.

It wasn't just forgetting the dinner that upset me. I felt as though my wife forgot me. I could have given her a guilt trip and made her feel worse about it, but I chose to offer Lysandra grace. I said, it'll be fine. It's okay. I forgave her and released her from the guilt of her offense. It took divine grace and wisdom for me to respond this way, it not natural for me, but with God all things are possible.

Told You So

When you are right you naturally want to say those ever-temping words, "I told you so!" It's in your nature to want to point out when you knew something was going to happen, good or bad. It's part of your humanity to want to broadcast when you're right. But remember, it's okay to be right and tell no one.

It's also in your nature to be tempted to shed light on your spouse's flaws. We sometimes joke around with each other by forcing the loser in an argument to say, "You were right; I was wrong." The reality is, you don't have to point out every time your spouse messes up. Hearing them admit fault should not bring you joy. They don't need you to magnify their faults. You are not tasked with reminding them of their mistakes.

Wisdom gives grace. Wisdom overlooks mistakes and minimizes faults.

Lysandra

I had an opportunity to overlook a mistake of Thomas's just yesterday. We have been on vacation and ended it with a day in New York City. We walked all over that impressive city. By the end of the day, we all had blisters on our feet, were hot, tired, and hungry. We wanted to eat at a specific pizza place in a remodeled church just a few blocks from Times Square. Little did we know, we were so close to this restaurant when Thomas led us in the other direction. We walked and walked to the wrong pizza place. Then we had to retrace our steps back through Times Square to the restaurant we were looking for.

I wanted to say "I told you so" or complain about my feet, but I chose not to say anything and to overlook my husband's error. There would be no wisdom in pointing out his mistake or in trying to make him feel worse about his navigational blunder. It would be petty to magnify it. So, I kept my mouth shut and offered grace to my Love. We all enjoyed our meal because we overlooked the offense and chose to have fun.

Start Today

Today can be a new beginning for you and your spouse. Extend grace over petty offenses, choose to overlook mistakes, and minimize flaws. This is the one you promised to love and cherish forever. Live that out by giving grace when offended.

Make it Personal:

1. Share three ways you see God's grace in your life.

2. Share a time you said, "I told you so." How was it received?

3. Describe a time when your spouse let go of a petty offense for you.

4. What petty offense or mistake do you need to let go of for your spouse?

5. How will you remind yourself to offer grace the next time your spouse makes a mistake?

Day 20: Proverbs Chapter 20

Marriage Goal: Put work into your marriage relationship.

*"The sluggard does not plow in the Autumn;
he will seek at harvest and have nothing."*

Proverbs 20:4

You Can't Reap What You Don't Plant

A successful farmer during this time understood how crucial it was to think ahead and work diligently. Farmers in Israel would plow their fields in late October to ensure the soil was prepared for planting in early November. This was the most beneficial time to plant because November marked the beginning of the rainy season, which was vital to the success of their crops.

If they missed planting by the rainy season, they were almost guaranteed to go hungry when April came around, which was the beginning of harvest season for them. This was a powerful warning to them to think ahead and to get to work. We are wise to heed this warning as well. The future is coming—whether we're prepared for it or not.

Thomas

Lysandra and I agreed that we would continually and intentionally work on our relationship before we got married. After marriage, we purposefully developed our relationship, even though we had four small children. We knew if we let the kids consume us, we wouldn't have any relationship to enjoy once they were all grown and gone. We understand that our future, most likely, includes years of an empty nest. We want to enjoy those years together and, based on the work we've put into our marriage, I believe we will!

Prepare the Soil

You are currently creating a crop in your marriage that you will harvest later. When you work on your relationship, you are plowing the field of your relationship. You are preparing the soil. Every time you put down your phone, make eye contact with your spouse, and work on your communication, you are plowing those fields. When you go on a date with your spouse each week you are preparing your relationship fields to be planted.

As you serve your spouse by cooking, cleaning, mowing, working a job, helping with the kids, grocery shopping, or helping them achieve their goals, you are planting seeds in your relationship field. When you are kind and tell them you love them, value them, and appreciate them, you are planting a harvest. Every time you make time to be sexual with your spouse, you are investing in a future harvest. Put in the work now; you will thank yourself later.

Lysandra

Currently, we have four teenage daughters in our home. They keep us very busy with their school, extra-curriculars, sports, and social lives; however, they are not our entire world. We take time away from our kids to intentionally invest in our marriage. We work on this relationship because we see its value. We date, talk, laugh, walk, and work together. All of this is sowing a harvest we will reap now and later. I look forward to our future together. We've been working on our relationship for so many years we just keep getting closer; our future is bright!

Laziness Has a Price

You may decide all of this is just more work than you're willing to do. You can't be bothered with this much effort. Maybe you never decided to check out of your marriage and coast, but now that you're faced with the idea of working on your relationship, you realize you've been coasting for a while. If you don't make a change and begin putting in the work, you will not have anything to harvest later. Your relationship will die out.

Giving into your laziness has a high cost. Your marriage may not last, and you may end up alone. If your marriage survives and you're not putting in the effort, you may be stuck in a lackluster partnership where both are numb—maybe even miserable. Make the change today, stop being lazy in your marriage, and put in the work; it will be worth it in the future. Wisdom prepares for the future by working hard now.

Make it Personal:

1. How did you work on your relationship before you got married

2. In what areas of your marriage have you been coasting?

3. Share with your spouse an area of your marriage where you feel like they have been coasting.

4. Is there a season you've been waiting to pass before you start working harder on your marriage?

5. List the ways you will work harder on your marriage relationship.

Day 21: Proverbs Chapter 21

Marriage Goal: Create a peaceful environment in your home.

"It is better to live in a corner of the housetop than in a house shared with a quarrelsome wife. 19 It is better to live in a desert land than with a quarrelsome and fretful woman."

Proverbs 21:9, 19

Your Sanctuary

Your home is the place where you were meant to come to for peace and rest. Your home is intended to be a sanctuary for you and for all who live there. A sanctuary is a place of refuge or safety, offering protection and peace. It is a safe and calm environment where someone feels at ease. A sanctuary provides a sense of security and calm, whether it's through physical protection or emotional comfort. Sounds nice, right?

Does this describe your home? If this is not how you feel in your home, it would be wise to evaluate why not. What is preventing your home from being this sanctuary of peace and refuge of protection?

The Tone of Your Home

It's interesting to note the thrust of these verses being directed at the woman in the home. Certainly, a man can be argumentative and quarrelsome, but the wife is the one who seems to be warned specifically in reference to the home here. There is something to be said about the tone in a home being set by the wife. Mom is typically the one who runs the home, the schedule, and the whole family.

Think about when you were a child; most likely when you said you were going to your grandparents' house, you probably said you were going to Grandma's. Commonly, we say we are going to our aunt's house or our mom's house. Yes, Dad is there with Mom, Uncle lives with Auntie too, and Grandpa calls it his home as well, but we normally view the home as the woman's domain. It's not about chauvinism; it's about who usually takes charge of the home environment—usually it's the wife.

So, it's not that the wife is taking all the heat here in Proverbs chapter 21, but it is understood that the tone of the home is most likely set by the woman. Women have a lot of power and influence over the home. That is a great honor for women, but also a great responsibility.

Thomas

Lysandra has taken these verses to heart from the very beginning of our marriage. She has been extremely thoughtful and deliberate in creating a peaceful environment in our home for our family to enjoy. Just yesterday we were lying in bed when I noticed our four daughters relaxing and laughing in the family room next to our bedroom. I turned to Lysandra and thanked her for creating this space we call home. I thanked her for making our home peaceful and comfortable for all of us. I reminded Lysandra that it was because of her that we all love coming home.

Lysandra

When the kids were little, I only worked in short seasons or short shifts to mainly be a stay-at-home mom. I loved it while it lasted. Being able to stay home with your children while they're young is a great privilege that not everyone gets to enjoy. Now the girls are older, and our financial situation is such that I must work outside the home. Whether working inside the home or outside; the home is my domain, and I set the tone for it.

I purposefully work to make the environment in our home quiet, clean, organized, and harmonious. I desire our home to be a safe place, not only physically, but emotionally too. I do my part to make it a sanctuary, but Thomas puts in effort as well. I couldn't do it without him. He makes sure everyone is protected. He brings a sense of safety from outside intruders but also safety to those who live in our home from one another. Our home is a safe place to share emotions and be authentic.

It takes both partners working together to accomplish this sanctuary of peace and safety.

You Affect Your Home

It takes two spouses to build a peaceful home, but it only takes one to destroy it. Your spouse can be working hard to create a peaceful, safe space for your family, but if you aren't on board, they will fail. Your spouse can be as sweet as pie and servantly as Mother Teresa, but if you are argumentative and quarrelsome, it doesn't matter how hard they try, you will ruin the environment of your home.

You must both agree that you will work together to be kind and tenderhearted, so that your home will be a peaceful place. You must both choose to be agreeable and refuse to be quarrelsome. If you are cantankerous, hot-tempered, and confrontational, the writer of Proverbs says it's better for your spouse to live in a dry desert or in an uncomfortable corner of a housetop. What contribution are you bringing to your relationship and environment? How are you affecting your home's tone?

There is great comfort in having a serene environment at home. Be a wise spouse who contributes to the peace and harmony of your family.

Make it Personal:

1. On a scale of 1 to 10, how peaceful is your home?

2. What would you like to change about your family's environment?

3. What are the best things about your home physically?

4. What are the best things about your home emotionally?

5. In what ways can you change to be less argumentative and quarrelsome?

Day 22: Proverbs Chapter 22

Marriage Goal: Have financial integrity.

*"The rich rules over the poor, and the borrower is the slave of the
lender. 9, "Whoever has a bountiful eye will be blessed,
for he shares his bread with the poor."*

Proverbs 22:7, 9

"Acceptable" Debt

In our culture today, it is quite normal to have significant debt. It's
perfectly acceptable in our world to have several credit cards, two or
three car loans, home equity loans, student debt, and a sizable
mortgage. Just because it's accepted, doesn't mean it's how God
intended for you to live. Your loving Heavenly Father knew that when
you are in debt, you are a slave to it. He doesn't want you to live in
slavery to anything, not addiction, not sin, and certainly not debt. God
wants you to live in freedom.

Debt is not a loner, and it brings a lot of baggage. When you have debt,
you also have stress, anxiety, guilt, frustration, fear, and resentment. It
may feel like that purchase or upgrade is worth the debt, but it usually
isn't. You may get the new luxury you wanted, but with it comes the
negative emotions listed above. Wisdom says, "Wait, save, be patient."
You don't need everything you want at the very moment you want it.
This is countercultural but true; waiting is healthy.

Debt Affects Your Marriage

As you can imagine, the negative emotions that come with debt are
going to affect your marriage. If you and your spouse are experiencing
stress, anxiety, guilt, frustration, fear, and resentment, your marriage is

under intense strain. You cannot have all this tension weighing on you and have a thriving marriage.

Thomas

Lysandra and I never intended to get into debt. In fact, we made a debt-free pact before we got married. We aimed to incur zero debt, other than our house payment. We were able to keep the pact until I became a full-time pastor, and she became a full-time Christian school teacher. Month after month, the credit card balance increased until it was maxed out. We were now incurring interest. We didn't always have money for food. To say that the debt negatively affected our marriage was an understatement.

I wanted to provide for my wife and little girls, but there just wasn't enough money, even though we lived a simple life. Lysandra's birthday was approaching and there was not enough on the credit card to buy her a present. Then a new credit card offer came in the mail; it seemed like the answer was right in front of me. I secretly opened a new credit card. It did alleviate some of the tension in our marriage—for a while.

The secret came out in the most embarrassing way possible. When we moved and were attempting to buy a house, in a new state, we had to undergo a credit check. We were sitting in the lender's office when the list of our debt was being assessed. When the loan officer mentioned my secret credit card, I listened as my wife argued with her that it was wrong; we didn't have that credit card. I finally fessed up in this stranger's office. It was humiliating and shameful as I watched the light in my wife's eyes go dark. She was devastated at my dishonesty. Trust me when I say, debt only causes more problems.

Lysandra

I've long forgiven Thomas for his secret credit card; I understand his motive for getting it. That credit card set us back financially. It felt like the hole we were digging out of dug deeper, as though we may never again see the light of day. I was crushed by the extra weight of the surprise debt, but more so by my husband's dishonesty. Thomas has never done anything like that again. He is completely honest in his conduct and wise in his spending. This has brought a lot of trust and confidence in him. I'm happy to say that now, due to our mutual commitment of living within our means and giving faithfully to God, we have zero debt (other than our mortgage).

Get to Give

We often think that the best reason to obtain more money, get that promotion, or earn a higher salary is to acquire more savings and retirement or to buy more stuff. While we believe strongly in preparing for the future by saving and building your retirement fund, that should not be a Christian's primary reason for earning more money. We see in Ephesians and Proverbs that the real reason to get is to give.

Look at what Paul says about it in Ephesians 4:28, *"Let the thief no longer steal, but rather let him labor, doing honest work with his own hands, so that he may have something to share with anyone in need."*

Your goal in your financial gain should be to bless others with it. You should find true joy in giving to those in need. It should make you happy to support missions and charities. You should be cheerful as you give to support your local church. You and your marriage are blessed when you are happy to give. Commit to each other to have financial integrity today.

Make it Personal:

1. Talk about your finances and list all debt.

2. How does it make you feel to have this amount of debt?

3. Apologize and take ownership of your part in your financial situation.

4. What are your joint financial goals?

5. How can you give more?

Day 23: Proverbs Chapter 23

Marriage Goal: Be genuinely generous.

"Do not eat the bread of a man who is stingy; do not desire his delicacies, 7 for he is like one who is inwardly calculating. "Eat and drink!" he says to you, but his heart is not with you. 8 You will vomit up the morsels that you have eaten and waste your pleasant words."

Proverbs 23:6–8

Marital Generosity

There are numerous ways to be generous in your marriage. Your spouse has many needs and wants, and you have the opportunity to meet them. Every spouse needs love, care, food, clothing, sex, shelter, faithfulness, and safety. Think of your spouse's specific needs; you have multiple opportunities to meet these needs.

Every spouse has wants and desires. Every spouse wants to be appreciated, remembered, considered, to have fun, pleasure, and gifts. Think of your spouse's specific wants; you have multiple opportunities every day to fulfill them.

Generosity doesn't keep score. Generosity has nothing to do with giving equal amounts as you get and everything to do with giving without thought for yourself. Marital generosity isn't meant to be conditional or perfectly equal. So often in marriage, we keep score. We only want to give if we get something. If I spent twenty dollars then I'll give you that to spend. If you had time alone for two hours, then I get two hours for me. If you served me sexually, then I'll serve you sexually. Check the marital scoreboard. If it's on, there's a problem.

Lysandra

Thomas is crazy generous. I know how blessed I am to be married to him. He gives and takes no thought for what he has received from me. He is just happy when I'm happy. I remember a time near my birthday when we had very little money. I told him I didn't want any birthday presents this year. I explained that if he got me a gift, I would be more anxious and upset about finances than if he just skipped getting me anything.

On my birthday, he came down the stairs with a present wrapped like a five-year-old got a hold of tape and a newspaper. I knew immediately he wrapped it. I got mad right away! "I told you not to buy me anything! We don't have any money, now I'm more stressed out than before—and it's my birthday!" When I finally shut up, he explained he used money he had saved from other people for his birthday four months ago.

I was so touched, I instantly started crying. He was so generous without hesitation or expectation of anything in return. His generosity continues to impress me to this day.

Genuine or Insincere

The example of generosity given to us in Proverbs Chapter 23 shows a calculating, fake, and manipulative person. This person shows no genuine desire to be generous. It's all about what they can get out of the other person. Their heart is not in it, and they are working an angle. If you receive anything from this person, you will soon regret it. This is not how God intended your marriage to be. Your spouse should never wonder if they'll regret getting something from you. Your spouse should never be fearful of "paying for" whatever you do for them.

Thomas

There is nothing in this world that makes me happier than making Lysandra happy. Watching her face light up when I give her something is the best feeling ever. My goal is to be generous in various ways. I enjoy buying her things, but I also love to give her my time, my attention, my love, and my help. I am not a natural servant. I must work at it. Being generous with my help is something I'm decisively, actively improving.

Acts of service is my wife's primary love language. I force myself to move quickly when I see ways I can help Lysandra. She is independent and moves quickly. There are times I know she wants help, but she won't wait for me—I have to hurry to be generous with my help. This takes discipline. You may not be naturally generous with your spouse in certain ways, but you can always learn and grow in your generosity.

Generosity Takes Many Forms

Most people think of generosity as buying presents. Marital generosity is much more than that and comes up in every aspect of your relationship.

You can be generous with your kind words and positive affirmations. You can be generous with your time, attention, and devotion. You can be generous with service, favors, and household chores. You can be generous in the bedroom with sexual gifts, boundless time, and an adventurous spirit. You can be generous with their personal space by allowing them to spend time with their friends, family and hobbies. You can be generous by offering them the space they need to accomplish what they're working toward in their career. You can be generous with your love by giving non-sexual back rubs, holding hands, hugs, and kisses.

Take your marital generosity to the next level. Astonish your spouse with your genuine generosity.

Make it Personal:

1. In what ways have you been keeping score in your relationship?

2. Share a time when your spouse was exceptionally generous.

3. In what ways do you feel you have been stingy in your relationship?

4. What aspect of generosity do you want to improve?

5. How do you feel when you see your spouse pleased by your generosity?

Day 24: Proverbs Chapter 24

Marriage Goal: Never give up on each other.

"For the righteous falls seven times and rises again,
but the wicked stumble in times of calamity."

Proverbs 24:16

Myth Busters

There is a myth out there that the perfect marriage exists. The truth is your marriage will never be perfect. The reason? You and your spouse will never be perfect. Your marriage is made up of two imperfect people; the result is an imperfect marriage. Take a moment to mourn the loss of hope for the perfect marriage.

"The righteous falls seven times." This verse implies that everyone makes mistakes. No matter how good a person is, they're still human.

You will fail at this marriage thing—so will your spouse. You both will act stupidly. You will speak carelessly. You will let one another down. This is a reality to accept, not to fight. This is why it's so imperative to be quick to forgive. Both parties in a marriage must be allowed to make mistakes and be human. It would be wise for each spouse to accept that you will fail your spouse, and your spouse will fail you.

Thomas

We have people who tell us frequently that we're so lucky because we have a "perfect" marriage. We reply the same way every time, "We don't have a perfect marriage, and luck has nothing to do with it. We are both selfish and make mistakes. We are each deeply flawed individuals. We have both failed so many times. Despite all of that, we never gave up, although we both thought about it more than once."

We have worked hard at our relationship for six years prior to walking down the aisle and for twenty-one years since. Our marriage still has its ups and downs, but it's stronger than it was in the beginning. Lysandra and I wrote a book entitled *Happily Never After* to show people that every marriage struggles but can improve through Jesus.

Lower the White Flag

The key is, when you fail, don't stay there. When you make a mistake, don't indulge in a pity party. When your spouse fails, don't give up on them. Just because one (or both) of you have a misstep, don't raise the white flag and surrender. When you or your spouse does something careless, don't throw in the towel. Get up and fight for marriage—it's worth it!

When you said, "Till death do us part," you meant it. Your spouse is counting on you to stay. It will be difficult, but you can do it with God's help. *"The righteous falls seven times and rises again."* No matter how many times you or your spouse fall, get back up again; that's what makes a follower of Jesus so special. Jesus followers aren't superhuman and perfect. What makes a Jesus-follower so unique isn't that they never fail; it's that they never fail to get up.

Don't Stay in Abuse

As a note, we aren't encouraging anyone to stay in an abusive marriage. Please don't misunderstand what we're saying. We want you to fight for an imperfect marriage. We don't want you to just keep taking abuse. Abuse is never what God intended, and he didn't design marriage to be torture from one spouse to another. Abuse is never okay. If you're in an abusive situation, please find support, get to safety, and get your children to safety.

Lysandra

Thomas and I know you probably have considered walking away from your marriage, or at least thought that it might be easier than sticking it out. We know this because we are both followers of Jesus who believe in the sanctity of marriage being forever, yet we have both thought about divorce. We never threatened it or spoke it, and we never pursued it, but the thought has been there once or twice.

Neither of us stayed in our "bad marriage" because of our commitment to one another. We stayed in our bad marriage because of our commitment to God and to marriage itself. We have a high value of marriage. God designed it, and He intended it to be "Till death do us part." Therefore, when we fall, we keep getting back up again.

I'm grateful we didn't give up when times were tough, because now we have such a great marriage—not perfect, but great! I love Thomas so deeply, and I absolutely love being married to him. If we had given up the first time we messed up, then we wouldn't be enjoying the wonderful marriage that we have now.

Never Give Up

It may seem easier to leave this marriage and find someone who treats you better, is more fun, follows Jesus closer, or is a better person. Staying married is hard; finding someone new is also hard. Sticking with it is hard; starting over is also hard. Accepting your spouse's shortcomings is hard; dealing with someone's new shortcomings is also hard. Choose your hard.

Choose to stay in the marriage as God designed—believe in it and work on it. If you work on your marriage, you won't be doing it alone. God will help you. Don't fall and stay there, get back up. Fight for your marriage. Never give up!

Make it Personal:

1. How have you idealized the perfect marriage?

2. In what ways would you like to see your marriage improve?

3. Share a time you thought about giving up on your relationship.

4. What has made you stay in your marriage up to this point?

5. How will you fight for your marriage this week?

Day 25: Proverbs Chapter 25

Marriage Goal: Appropriately comfort one another.

"Whoever sings songs to a heavy heart is like one who takes off a garment on a cold day, and like vinegar on soda."

Proverbs 25:20

We're in This Together

One of the best parts of marriage is knowing that you'll never face life alone. There is such reassurance in handling every situation together as a team. Life throws many random challenges at you. You will experience outstanding joy—and devastating tragedy. There will be enormously high highs and horribly low lows. You will feel moments of great confidence and moments you don't have any idea what to do. It's tough not knowing what is going to come when. Life can change in a single moment and leave you in shock.

When life throws you one of these curveballs, your teammate is right there with you. The question to consider today is this, what kind of a teammate are you?

Your spouse needs your comfort when sorrow comes. Additionally, they need your celebration when they experience great victory. They need your help—even when you're swamped. They need your presence when they're lonely. They need you to be emotionally present. It would be wise to frequently examine yourself in this area of emotional maturity.

An emotionally mature person can sense when someone hurts and responds appropriately. A wise spouse knows to be quiet and just be there when their partner is devastated. An emotionally present

144

husband or wife understands the importance of matching their spouse's outlook. A sensitive person will comfort in a meaningful way.

Thomas

I learned early on in our relationship not to accuse Lysandra of being too sensitive. First of all, it's not true. Secondly, who gets to determine the exact amount of sensitivity for each individual? And most of all, it only makes a wife more upset to be told they are being too sensitive.

To be honest, I'm not naturally empathetic; I had to develop my sensitivity. I had to progress in my sympathy through a lot of effort, and it took years to cultivate my emotional intelligence. Having a wife and four daughters certainly helped the process. If you're not overly emotional like me, don't use that as an excuse to not be there for your spouse the way you should be. Keep working at it. Grow in your emotional maturity. It is wise to understand emotions.

Lysandra

Thomas is my go-to for comfort. I know I can call him, text him, or cry on his shoulder when I'm upset. It seems like he knows just what to say to make me feel better. He knows when all I need is to be held, he is the first person I call to share good news with. He is my person, and I trust the way he interacts with me. I'm thankful for him, and I work hard to be the comforter he needs—in the ways he needs.

Marriage Poison

If your spouse is weeping and comes to you for comfort and you laugh, you have no emotional wisdom. You are poisoning your marriage if you are emotionally unaware. As our verse for today states, it's like taking off their winter coat in the middle of winter, which feels miserable, or when you pour vinegar over baking soda which causes an explosive reaction. Being comforted inappropriately feels terrible. Having an improper response to something you share with your spouse feels awful.

Pay attention to your spouse's emotions. Make intelligent decisions about how to comfort them in meaningful ways. When you can master your emotional responses, you are emotionally wise.

Make it Personal:

1. How do you feel knowing you face everything as a team?

2. Describe a time you weren't comforted the way you felt you needed.

3. What has been your highest high?

4. What has been your lowest low?

5. Share how your spouse can comfort you appropriately.

Day 26: Proverbs Chapter 26

Marriage Goal: Be honest with your motives and intentions.

*"Like a madman who throws firebrands, arrows, and death 19 is the
man who deceives his neighbor and says, "I am only joking!"*

Proverbs 26:18–19

You're "Crazy"

In 1944, a movie was made about a man who convinced his wife she
was crazy every time she became suspicious of him or caught him in a
lie. The movie is called *Gaslight* because one of his deceptions was
convincing her the gaslight wasn't flaring up and down—when in reality,
it was. This is where we get the modern term, *gaslighting*.

Our verse for today expresses how detrimental it is to be close to
someone who is deceptive. Rather than owning their duplicity, they try
to convince you that you're crazy. They convince you that they were
only kidding when they said hurtful words or acted inconsiderately.
They say they were joking when they hurt your feelings.

Their goal is to avoid responsibility for their actions. They want the
freedom to do and say what they want without the restriction of
considering any repercussions. They can't be bothered by another
person's feelings. They are selfish and unloving.

I'm Just Joking

The example we see in our passage today is someone who uses the
excuse they were "joking" whenever they want to get out of trouble.
It's okay to joke around if both parties agree that it's funny. If it isn't
funny to them but rather hurtful, it isn't a joke, it's an insult. You can't
joke with someone, hurt their feelings, and then tell them you're

guiltless because it was a joke. You're not funny; you're mean. Being mean isn't only a character flaw, it's a sin. We are told numerous times in Scripture to be kind and loving. To ignore these commands is sinful.

It's not okay to use the excuse "I'm just joking" as a free pass to deceive or be unkind.

Lysandra

It is critical in marriage to draw boundary lines. If your spouse doesn't know where the boundaries are, they can't stay inside them. I'll never forget the first time Thomas crossed my invisible boundary line. I was only sixteen and hadn't shared where the line was at this point in our relationship.

Thomas and I were on a snowy Iowa walk in the beginning of January. He made a joke about me being warm because I was thick. He was totally and completely joking but it cut me so deeply. He was unaware of my bodily insecurities, so it wasn't malicious. Once I shared with him how I felt, he knelt in the snow and begged for my forgiveness. I forgave him right away, but he insisted on freezing his knees in the snow for a significant time as his penance. That was the first, and last time, he teased me about my weight.

Thomas

I've always been a flirt and take great joy in teasing Lysandra. Joking around and having fun is one way I show love to my wife. I will always tease Lysandra, but I will never cross the boundary lines she has drawn. I love her too much to hurt her that way. I want her to trust me and feel safe with me. If I am consistently hurting her with my teasing, it's not fun, it's mean.

Be Honest

If you were deceptive or mean, own it. Admit that you were wrong and say the words, "I'm sorry." Admit that you took it too far and hurt your spouse. Apologize for your thoughtlessness. Be honest about your motives and intentions. Don't hide behind excuses. Be real and strong enough to admit when you are wrong. This is wisdom.

Make it Personal:

1. Has there been a time you tried to convince your spouse they were crazy when you were wrong?

2. Has there been a time when you tried to convince your spouse you were joking when you were really being mean?

3. Share your boundaries for teasing.

4. Describe a time you crossed one of your spouse's known boundaries.

5. Own and apologize for any times you used, "I was only joking" as an excuse.

Day 27: Proverbs Chapter 27

Marriage Goal: Speak the truth—with love.

"Better is open rebuke than hidden love. 6 Faithful are the wounds of a friend; profuse are the kisses of an enemy."

Proverbs 27:5–6

Courage to Speak Truth

All relationships fall into categories based on how shallow or deep they are. Categories include stranger, acquaintance, friend, close friend, confidant, and best friend. Relationships will flow throughout these categories over time. Think of your best friend in college, it is quite unusual if that person remains your best friend today. Just because a relationship moves deeper doesn't mean it will stay there. That same relationship can become shallow again over time. Relationships evolve and devolve, according to the level of intimacy, truth, trust, and interaction.

There are many factors to a relationship's evolution such as time spent, communication, connection, intentionality, and shared interests. One of the most significant factors to a relationship growing is the permission to speak truth into one another's lives. A friendship where both parties are free to speak truth, even when it's difficult to say and hard to hear, is a friendship that will grow into a deep and meaningful bond.

A close, meaningful relationship is one where you have the courage and resolve to speak truth to your spouse even when it's difficult. When you see an issue arise in your spouse's life, say something. If you notice your partner having angry outbursts and it's becoming a pattern, tell them the truth. If you see your spouse has neglected time with God for a season, speak up. When your spouse engages in gossip, don't join in, but point it out to them.

True love doesn't sit by quietly and watch their loved one destroy their life. If you are in a close relationship, you will make the hard choice to speak the hard truth. You do this because your spouse is valuable to you. You do this because they are worth an uncomfortable conversation. Be careful to pick and choose when to speak, based on how serious the matter is. Don't use this as an opportunity to become a giant nag. Speak up if it's important. Be quiet if it's not.

Thomas

I really love Lysandra. I never want to hurt her, but it is my love for her that is willing to hurt her if necessary. I care enough about her to tell her when something is causing her to go the wrong direction. There was a time when I could see she was filling up her schedule too full. She has always packed her life with good, even as a teenager, but this time was different. The number of "good things" she strived to fit in were clearly affecting her health. She was hurting herself. I knew she didn't want to hear me tell her this truth, but my love for her trumped my desire for her to be happy with me.

I carefully chose a time and told her she needed to back out of something. She didn't like hearing this and bargained with me for a few minutes, but in the end, she knew it was true. She had already felt it, and she needed me to say it. Your spouse needs you to say something when you see something.

Permission to Speak Freely

If you want to strengthen your relationship and see it grow, you not only must speak the difficult truths, but you must also be willing to hear them. Have you given your spouse verbal permission to speak truth into your life? Your spouse may not know if they haven't heard you say the words. They may feel uneasy about bringing up hard conversations with you. Or worse yet, they may be afraid of your reaction. If you reacted poorly to them telling truth in the past, they most likely learned their lesson and know you don't want to hear it. They will shut down; your relationship will be stunted or devolve.

You have the power to change the course of your relationship by simply being open to reproof and correction. The insecure person is the one who cannot handle the truth that hurts. It shows great maturity to listen to someone's wise correction. It's hard and it's uncomfortable, but in the end, you will be a better person for it and your relationship will be stronger. The truth really will set you free.

Lysandra

Thomas and I have given each other verbal permission to speak truth into each other's lives. We're careful how we do it. Typically, when I feel the need to confront Thomas about something difficult, yet true, it sounds something like this:

"Honey, you know how much I love you; you are an awesome husband to me and a fantastic father to the girls. I've noticed something in you lately that concerns me. It feels like you've been a little extra harsh with the girls. Is there something that's been bothering you? Is there a way that I can help? I appreciate you being faithful to discipline our kids and make them mind. You really are an excellent father, and I'm blessed to have you as my teammate."

This was a real conversation I had with Thomas a long time ago. I wanted him to hear the truth but also to sense the love that I have for him. We bring up difficult conversations, but we're extremely mindful of how we do so.

It's How You Said It

The way you speak truth is crucial to how it is received. Your spouse will not be interested in what you say unless you show how much you care. Prove you love them genuinely by speaking truth in the most loving way you possibly can. Be gentle, not harsh. Be kind, not mean. Be tender, not hardened.

You can have the purest motives and the most important truth to share, but if it comes out the wrong way, it will not be heeded. Truth in love means a gentle tone, wise timing, and carefully constructing the conversation. Having difficult conversations in loving ways will create a marriage that is so strong it can last forever.

Make it Personal:

1. How deep do you feel your marriage is?

2. Share a time you wish you would have said something to your spouse but didn't.

3. Describe a time someone shared a hard truth with you.

4. What makes truth seem loving to you?

5. Give your spouse permission right now to speak truth into your life.

Day 28: Proverbs Chapter 28

**Marriage Goal: Be transparent about
sin struggles and turn from sin.**

*"Whoever conceals his transgressions will not prosper, but he who
confesses and forsakes them will obtain mercy."*

Proverbs 28:13

Missing the Mark

It can be so difficult to admit you messed up. It feels shameful to admit
your own wrongdoing. The word the Bible uses in today's Scripture is
transgression or *sin*. Sin is breaking God's rules, and not measuring up
to His requirements. Sin is missing the mark. We see from Scripture that
every person has sinned. Paul makes it clear in Romans 3:23, *"For all
have sinned and fall short of the glory of God."* You are not immune to
sin, and neither is your spouse.

Often in marriage we want to pretend we don't have sin. We hide our
sin struggles from our spouse thinking there's no need for them to
know. We think our shortcomings don't need to be shared with anyone,
they are private. We believe they are personal. Secret sin will slowly
wreck you. Hidden wrongdoing destroys marriage. There is no wisdom
in hiding your sin.

Why We Conceal Sin

There are many reasons you may not admit your sin:

- You deceived yourself that it isn't sin.
- You convinced yourself that your sin isn't hurting you or anyone
  else.
- You love your sin and want to keep practicing it.

- You have become so accustomed to it that it doesn't bother you anymore, your conscience is numb.
- You don't care that it's wrong.
- You keep telling yourself you'll stop soon, so nobody needs to know.
- You think your spouse will leave you if they know the truth.
- You want to appear "good."
- Your sin is addicting, and you don't want your spouse to know your weakness.
- You're afraid your spouse will make you get help for your sin struggle.
- You simply enjoy it, and you want to continue to indulge in it.

These are just a few of the many reasons people don't tell the truth about their sin.

Confess

Our Proverb for today shows us that confessing our transgression is the first wise step toward prosperity and mercy. James says it this way in James 5:16, *"Therefore, confess your sins to one another and pray for one another, that you may be healed. The prayer of a righteous person has great power as it is working."*

If you have a sin you are struggling with right now, it's time to tell your spouse. Confess it to them. Everything you do affects them, especially your sin. They need to know so they can be privy to every area of your life. They also may be able to help encourage you to do right. Your spouse can give you gentle reminders when you head down that road again. Most importantly, your spouse can pray for you like no one else, because they love you like no one else.

Lysandra

Confession is difficult. It's embarrassing. It's never fun, but it's freeing. When our daughters were young, it was easy for me to speak to them in a way that I knew wasn't pleasing to the Lord. I was around them twenty-four seven—I was often exhausted. I homeschooled all four of them, and the hardest part of homeschooling isn't the math or English, it's getting your kids to do their work. The most difficult thing about homeschooling is the discipline.

One day I had had it with their disobedience. I lost it and yelled out, "Do your schoolwork now!" I was loud and scary. My girls were in shock! They all straightened right up, grabbed their pencils, and started working. Unfortunately, my yelling worked. So, I did it again the next day, and the next. I found myself in a pattern. I was ashamed of my behavior, which had now become common in our home during school hours.

God spoke to my heart about my yelling. I wasn't okay with my sinful behavior. At our next family meeting I confessed my sin to my family. I apologized for it and explained that I was working with God to change my behavior. Later in private, I asked Thomas to remind me if he heard me yell at the kids again. He agreed he would help me with my sin struggle. There was freedom in owning my sin and confessing it to my family.

Forsake

Once the confession has been made there is another step to take. This is a step that can never be overlooked or skipped. You must forsake your sin. Forsaking sin is the idea of turning away from it, getting away from it, essentially ditching it. This means you will discontinue doing the wrong. This is making a commitment to God and to your spouse to change.

Forsaking sin requires prayer, personal resolve, and accountability. You especially need accountability if your sin has become an ongoing pattern of behavior—and now you have a bad habit you must break. It would be wise for you to make necessary changes, so you don't go near the place where you habitually sin. In Romans 13:14 Paul warns us to not give ourselves the opportunity to do wrong, *"But put on the Lord Jesus Christ, and make no provision for the flesh, to gratify its desires."*

Thomas

Forsaking sin is difficult. Discontinuing a bad habit is so tough. What's equally tough is beginning a good habit. I needed help forsaking a secret sin, and I knew Lysandra would help me. My sin struggle was one of neglect. I didn't need to stop doing something wrong; I needed to start doing something right. James 4:17 puts it this way, *"So whoever knows the right thing to do and fails to do it, for him it is sin."* It was a hidden sin because I'm a pastor and I couldn't advertise it; what would people think of me! I struggled to read my Bible every day. I struggled reading for the purpose of spending time with God and growing my faith. Yes, I studied for sermons practically every day, but personal time with Jesus is different and completely necessary.

I uncomfortably shared my sin struggle with my wife one day. After confessing my spiritual neglect, I told my wife I wanted to turn away from this and start fresh. I asked her to help me. She helps me with all other calendar and schedule-related items, so it just made sense that she could help me with this as well.

She began to ask me questions daily including:

- What passage did you read this morning?
- Did you remember to spend time alone with God this morning?
- What did God speak to you about in your morning devotion?

None of her questions were judgmental or meant to criticize. They were meant only to encourage me to stay on track. This created much-needed accountability for me. She helped me to forsake my sin of neglect.

Wise Way = Best Way

Living a life of wisdom isn't always easy. Sometimes it is very challenging, but doing the wise thing is always best for you and for your marriage. It is wise to be honest with yourself, your spouse, and God about your wrongdoing. Confess your sin and forsake it. You will have a right relationship with God and with your spouse when you do.

Make it Personal:

1. If you are hiding sin from your spouse, share it with them now.

2. Share a time your sin was neglecting something good.

3. Share a time your sin was doing something wrong.

4. Share ideas of how to help one another with each other's sin struggles.

5. Make a commitment now to turn away from your sin.

Day 29: Proverbs Chapter 29

Marriage Goal: Practice humility.

*"One's pride will bring him low,
but he who is lowly in spirit will obtain honor."*

Proverbs 29:23

What Pride?

The funny thing about pride is that usually you're too proud to see your own problem with pride. If you are prideful, it will undoubtably affect your marriage negatively.

If you are proud, you cannot open up and be vulnerable because that would require your spouse seeing the ugly parts of you. Your pride will not let that happen. This lack of vulnerability prohibits closeness. A proud spouse must always win. You have a "win-at-all-costs" attitude because the most important thing to you is you. This prevents conflict resolutions and create resentment.

If you struggle with pride, you are self-centered. You think about you first and measure every decision by how it will affect you, with little regard for how it will affect your spouse. Your pride is fuel for arguments and disagreements. As a person of pride, you deem your viewpoint the only right one, therefore you will fight over anything that goes against your perspective. Your pride deceives you into believing you are never wrong. Due to this, you don't say sorry or own your mistakes. You excuse them or deny they exist. This causes your spouse to become numb and check out of the relationship. As Proverbs tells us, *your pride will bring you low*. Your pride can ruin your marriage.

Lysandra

Pride has always been present in my life. I feel like I've been struggling with it my whole life. I can relate so deeply to the Apostle Paul when he wrote in Romans 7:15, *"For I do not do what I want, but I do the very thing I hate."* I hate pride, and I don't want it to be present anywhere in my life. Yet, every time I turn around, I catch myself doing the thing I hate, letting my pride rule me.

I see it everywhere in my life, but it pops up most frequently in my marriage. There are many times when I'm self-centered, arrogant, self-protective, selfish, and a know-it-all. I repeatedly ask God to humble my heart. I confess my pride to Him often and start over. I'm thankful for a God who is quick to forgive and capable of helping me change.

Thomas

I also struggle with pride. Having a marriage where one spouse struggles with pride is hard enough. It's tough if you both do. I'm naturally a confident guy and my confidence can cross the line into pride in an instant. One of my problems is knowing when that happens. If God or Lysandra points out my pride to me, I have a desire to change. I don't want to be prideful and alienate all my relationships. I am working on this; I want to grow.

It's crazy how my pride comes out in our marriage and affects our relationship. I see my pride put distance between me and Lysandra, and I hate it. Yet, before I know it, I've pushed her away again with my selfishness. God isn't done with me yet, and I'm thankful He hasn't given up on me. He is actively working in my life to help me stay humble.

Humility is Everything

A humble spirit will transform your marriage. C.S. Lewis masterfully defines humility, "Humility is not thinking less of yourself but thinking of yourself less."

Humility is essential for personal and relational growth. While pride screams, "I don't need to change!" humility quietly admits, "I have room to grow." You will never grow until you are humble enough to admit you're not perfect.

Humility brings satisfying compromise. When you have a humble spirit, you are open to compromise. You no longer need to win every argument and see the value in compromising with your spouse to find a middle ground. You understand you may be wrong. When you see you are wrong, you own it and apologize for it.

Humility causes you to listen to your spouse. Your humble spirit recognizes they have valuable thoughts, feelings, and perspectives. You have a genuine desire to hear what they have to say. You know you don't know it all and are open to changing your opinion.

Humility breeds gratitude. You understand through humility that you don't deserve the good you have. You greatly value your spouse and marriage. This leads you to be appreciative. You acknowledge your spouse for what they bring to the table and thank them for all they do—including loving you.

You will be greatly blessed if you can trade your pride for humility. It's ironic that the wiser you are, the humbler you are. Empty yourself of your pride to obtain wisdom and transform your relationship.

Make it Personal:

1. Share a time when you were prideful recently.

2. How does your pride come out in your marriage?

3. Describe a way your spouse is humble.

4. In what ways do you feel you need to grow personally?

5. Show your humility by appreciating your spouse for three ways they enhance your life.

Day 30: Proverbs Chapter 30

Marriage Goal: Be content.

*"Remove far from me falsehood and lying; give me neither poverty nor
riches; feed me with the food that is needful for me, 9 lest I be full and
deny you and say, "Who is the Lord?" or lest I be poor and steal and
profane the name of my God."*

Proverbs 30:8–9

Marital Contentment

Contentment is the state of being satisfied with what you have. It's easy
to become dissatisfied in your marriage and tempting to feel like it
could be better. If your spouse was more attentive, you'd be happy. If
you were closer, you'd be content. If you spent more quality time
together, life would be complete. You can convince yourself that the
only thing hindering contentment is if the marriage was just a bit better.

Your marriage is not the key to your happiness or your contentment.
Your own submission to God is. Contentment happens when
acceptance happens. Accept the spouse God gave you and submit to
the plan God has for your life; contentment will follow. Being content
in your marriage will bring a sweet freedom into your life.

Lysandra

There was a long season where I was discontented with our marriage.
Mostly, I was discontented with Thomas. I wanted him to work harder,
be nicer, lead spiritually, and be better all around. The most beautiful
thing happened when I gave up on him changing. He changed.

I had finally stopped nagging him. I stopped trying to manipulate him
into certain behaviors. I stopped trying to trick him into doing what I

thought was the right thing. I accepted him for who he was, shortcomings and all. I accepted my marriage as it was and began to focus on my own behavior. Once I chose contentment, my marriage improved.

Avoid Coasting

Being content doesn't mean you stop working on your relationship. It simply means that you live a life of acceptance with the state you are in, while still investing in the future. Contentment is not an excuse to coast the rest of your relationship, it is being at peace with what you have and working toward a better future. Never stop investing in your spouse; they are worth it.

Thomas

I've been content with our marriage from day one and never thought I could do better than Lysandra. I've known from before we got married that I hit the jackpot with her. Contentment was never my struggle. I was more likely to be lazy in our relationship and just coast. Once I had the woman I wanted, and I had the marriage I always wanted, I sat back for a while and just enjoyed it. I didn't always put in that much work. I needed to keep my contentment and add investment to it.

God Knows What You Need

God gifted you your spouse. Your marriage wasn't an accident. It's beautiful how the writer of this passage requests that God not give them too much or too little. He understood that God knows exactly what we need. He realized that if God gave him more than he needed he may turn away from God and believe he didn't need Him anymore. He also understood the opposite could also be equally detrimental. If God didn't give him enough, he may sin against God by seeking what he needed in dishonest ways. His prayer was one of submission to God's provision.

When was the last time you submitted to God's provision of your spouse in your life? Rest in the fact that God knew the spouse you needed. Accept the spouse God gifted you—submit to His plan for your life. Don't wish you had someone else or that your spouse would be more like someone else. Be content with who they are and who they are not. Contentment is ultimately trusting God for His provision.

Make it Personal:

1. Name three things you would like to change about your marriage.

2. Give those three things to God accepting how things are now.

3. Name three things you would like to change about your spouse.

4. Tell your spouse you love them for who they are and accept everything about them.

5. Pray together, thanking God for your spouse and for the marriage He has gifted you.

Day 31: Proverbs Chapter 31

Marriage Goal: Trust each other.

"An excellent wife who can find? She is far more precious than jewels. 11 The heart of her husband trusts in her, and he will have no lack of gain. 12 She does him good, and not harm, all the days of her life."

Proverbs 31:10–12

Striking Gold

It's like winning the lottery when you marry the right person. When you know you married the one God designed for you, it's like you struck gold. That person is more precious than all the gems and all the riches this world can offer. You know you have a treasure. Take a moment to truly value the person God gave you today. Thank God for them.

Tell your spouse how you're specifically thankful for them. Value your spouse as the gift God gave you and try to be a husband or wife worthy of this gift. Do good to your spouse as often as possible. Build a marriage built on trust.

Trust Level

When someone does only good to you, you trust them wholeheartedly. You are safe with them. How is your marital trust level?

Also, your spouse should feel complete safety with you in every way. If you have lost their trust, don't expect them to start trusting you automatically, just because you said sorry and made some promises. Earn their trust back slowly with repeated actions.

Someone once said, "Trust is lost in buckets and gained back in drops." It will take time, so be patient. Continue to earn their trust one drop at a time by doing what is trustworthy—day in and day out. If they begin to trust you again, don't take that for granted. Express your gratitude for their trust.

The reason the husband in this famous passage about marriage could trust his wife is because she did him only good. She earned his trust with years of goodness and faithfulness. There is great wisdom in her example.

Thomas

There was a time, early on in our marriage, when putting Lysandra before my own selfish desires was rare. My goal wasn't always to do good to her but to do what I wanted. Due to my years of selfishness, I lost a certain amount of her trust. She felt that she had to fight for herself and the kids for a long season. She couldn't trust my decisions were for their good rather than my own.

Once I saw this dynamic that I had created, I owned it and apologized. She was quick to forgive me, but she couldn't trust me right away. It took months of changed behavior to convince her that I wasn't living for myself. She still questioned decisions and was hesitant to follow at times. The trust I had lost was earned back slowly over many months. I proved to my wife that I was changing, not that I was perfect. That's when she could trust me again.

Now, we enjoy a pleasant, comfortable, content, and peaceful marriage full of trust.

Lysandra

I trust Thomas completely. I know his goal is to do good to me, and my heart safely trusts him. I believe he'll say only positive things about me and is a trustworthy confidant. I trust him to do kind things for me, and he is trustworthy in his commitment to our marriage vows. I have no reason to worry or doubt. He has earned my trust.

In turn, I want to be worthy of his trust. I do that by behaving in a way that earns and keeps his trust. I don't expect him to trust me, wisdom says I must prove that I am trustworthy by my words and actions.

The Wisest of All

If you want to understand how to be wise in your marriage, follow the wisest one of all. Follow Jesus. Your relationship with your spouse is a picture of Jesus and His followers. We are the bride of Christ. Ephesians 5:25 clearly lays out His example for us, *"Husbands, love your wives, as Christ loved the church and gave himself up for her."* Jesus is the perfect example of doing good and earning trust. He is the ultimate example of true love. Jesus's love for us was so boundless that He gave the greatest gift of all; He laid down His life and died for us. John 15:13 tells us that there is no greater demonstration of love for someone, *"Greater love has no one than this, that someone lay down his life for his friends."*

Jesus not only gave the ultimate sacrifice—death—but He lived His life sacrificially each day. He healed people. How can you help bring healing to your spouse? He took time for people when He was busy. How can you make time for your spouse? He fed people when they were hungry. How can you feed your spouse's soul? He helped people when He was in the middle of other work. How can you help your spouse, even when you are in the middle of your work? He comforted people in meaningful ways. How can your comfort your spouse? He gave people water to refresh them. How can your refresh your spouse's spirit? He provided all their needs. How can you provide for your spouse's needs?

If you want to do good to your spouse, as the book of Proverbs describes this wife doing for her husband, follow Jesus's example. He doesn't cause harm; He only does good to us.

God gave you the gift of your spouse and of your marriage. Cherish the gift of your marriage and value your person. This is wisdom.

Make it Personal:

1. Tell your spouse how grateful you are for them.

2. In what ways can you wholeheartedly trust your spouse?

3. Share an area with which you are reluctant to trust your spouse.

4. List three good things you will do for your spouse this week.

5. Thank God aloud for your spouse and your marriage.

Conclusion

This is only the beginning. Now that you and your spouse have walked through Proverbs together, you are better prepared for the next step to a wiser marriage relationship. This is the end of this book, but not the end of your journey to knowing God and better understanding His character.

Continue. Find another study that will keep both of you focused on God and His plan for your life. Your marriage is one of your most sacred gifts from your generous Father. Enjoy it, invest in it, treasure it. Continue to seek wisdom. Pursue it and you will find it. When you live according to wisdom in your marriage relationship, you will experience what only God can give—a joyous, content, peaceful, fulfilling marriage.

About Family Meeting

Our desire is to help you have the meaningful relationships that you desire in your marriage and family.

Thomas Osterkamp, Lead Pastor at Beachside Community Church in Palm Coast, FL, is married to his childhood sweetheart Lysandra. They have been serving God in pastoral ministry for over 25 years.

Lysandra and Thomas have four beautiful, spunky, funny girls: Kathryne, Isabella, Abigail, and Violet. Their house is always busy, dramatic, exciting, and full of love.

Additionally, *The Family Meeting Podcast* is a show all about family relationships, built to help you have the family dynamic that you want. Thomas and Lysandra invite you to be a part of their family. They pull back the curtain on their family life to share practical tips and advice on everything from marriage, parenting, sex, and everything in between. For helpful posts, videos, podcast show notes, or to book them to speak at your next event, visit www.familymeeting.org.

End Notes

[1] Christy Bieber, J.D., "Revealing Divorce Statistics in 2024," Forbes Advisor, Accessed on October 29, 2024, https://www.forbes.com/advisor/legal/divorce/divorce-statistics/

[2] R.C. Sproul, *The Purpose of God: Ephesians* (Ross-shire, Great Britain: Christian Focus, 2011), 125.

Made in the USA
Columbia, SC
25 November 2024

47052653R00102